JUST

"*Just Say Father* is a priceless ⸲ ... ...o are longing for a familiar friendship with *Father* God. It gives us an intimate, deeply personal glimpse into the heart of the infinite, personal God. I recommend it highly."

> —Richard J. Foster, author of several books including
> *Celebration of Discipline* and *Sanctuary of the Soul*

"*Just Say Father* touched me to the core. . . . I loved every word in it. This book will become a classic."

> —Victor Hashweh, Amman, Jordan

"*Just Say Father* authentically shares stories and examples that provide a much-needed reminder that as Abba's children, we don't have to work for *Father*'s love; we work *from* it. I'm personally grateful for Fred's literary contribution for translating spiritual information into practical application. Growing up with an adoptive father, never knowing my biological father, and then one day becoming a father required me to connect with *Father* to provide heavenly context to my earthly fathering experiences. If you could document almost everything you needed to know regarding *Father*, this is how you do it."

> —Montell Jordan, Multi-platinum, Grammy-nominated
> recording artist, Author & Pastor

"*Just Say Father* will affect the heart and soul of every reader with its spiritual significance—another beautiful and deeply inspiring book from Fred Hartley. He draws compelling lessons from a wide range of best-loved songs and films, and from his own personal life, and applies it to the largest lessons that all of us as sons and daughters, and as parents, can learn from the Bible and what he calls—in the most powerful and heartfelt phrase in this book—re-parenting in Jesus' name. As a childhood friend of Fred and as a professor of literature, I find this book speaks very personally to me as I have dear memories of our coming of age together and I love Fred's gifts as a storyteller and writer."

> —Thomas Gustafson, PhD, Associate Professor of English
> and American Studies, University of Southern California

"Fred Hartley is a visionary leader, marked by wisdom and passion. He is a great preacher, teacher, mentor and author of many spiritual books focused on encountering our heavenly *Father* through prayer. In *Just Say Father* he explains his personal intimacy with him and how to experience *Father*'s blessing. People are wandering under an orphan spirit and fatherlessness is a global crisis. Jesus expanded *Father*'s family and reflects the greatest love on earth. Being re-parented is essential to hearing and obeying *Father*. *Just Say Father* will be used to retrain the church—a must-read."

—Alex Alaro, Discipleship Training,
Ethiopian Kale Heywet Church

"Many of us realize Africa is a fatherless continent. After reading *Just Say Father*, I must say that our world is a fatherless world. Fred Hartley has a timely message for a hurting world. I read my dear friend Fred Hartley's book each morning, listening to the voice of the Spirit reteaching me about the amazing love of God my *Father* and saying to my *Father*: "*Father, re-parent me, in Jesus' name!*" God wants to raise a generation of spiritual fathers and mothers who will be a channel of an outpouring of love and compassion in the nations. *Just Say Father* is an explanation of that prophetic truth. I pray this Kingdom book will be adapted and translated in as many languages as possible."

—Daniel A.K.L Gomis, Regional Director,
Church of the Nazarene, Africa

"If you are someone who has never felt quite good enough—like there was something missing, like maybe God overlooked you—read this book. Every chapter. Every word. As a lifelong striver—the kind of person who hoped that every achievement, recognition, and milestone would prove that I was *finally* worthy—I found relief in the pages of the book. Fred Hartley taught me that not only does God love me just as I am, He created me to be just as I am. *Father* God is my perfect parent. And in Him I have access to all I need. In Him, I am *finally* enough. I could read and re-read every chapter of his book and continue to soak it up. The practice of being re-parented by God our *Father* is simply life-changing. Soak in every page. I promise, you will never be the same."

—Lee Hartley Carter, President and Partner,
Maslansky+Partners; Author, *Persuasion*

"In a world that labels people, where there is significant parental absence at home, Fred Hartley paints an unforgettable portrait of God as a *Father*—One who loves, heals, liberates and transforms. Fred opens our eyes to a vision of God as *Dad*. Anyone who yearns to grow in his relationship, intimacy and communion with *Father*, to appreciate him as a *Dad* who takes away from us anxiety, fear and depression, you will find this book life-changing."

—Juan Zuniga, Church Planter, Europe

"Fred Hartley takes us on a journey of healing to *Abba, Father*. Each chapter takes us deeper into the true relationship with *Father's* heart. I was penetrated by the idea of the father-wound—that we are striving for home. Being an orphan that lost her father before my fourth birthday, I always had a problem relating to the *Father* as my *Abba*. Being born and raised in the Palestinian society, as a girl, I felt loss even in common places. Reading this book has brought so many flashbacks and deep emotions. Reading this book is a must—a healing way to respond to *Father's* invitation. The orphan mentality is far more transcendent than simply lacking a relationship with your biological parents; it's about finding *Father*. This book will expose you to the idea that fatherlessness is more of a global crisis than we actually realize, and by the end of the book, you will be able to receive your re-birth and the security of being re-parented."

—Dr. Madeleine Sara, Founder, Women Empowerment Ministry, Jerusalem, Israel

"*Just Say Father* is very much a playbook for life, helping you under-stand the importance of one of the most critical connections all of us can have—connecting with both your father and *Father*. This is one of the most fulfilling, comforting, healing and purpose-building gifts anyone can have—one of the most powerful forces in your life. This book is a guide to better understand this important connec-tion; its meaning, its content and its healing power is not just useful on a personal level, but also a truly cathartic experience. It gave me permission to feel more deeply about something I always felt but often could not find the words to express. Whether you are seeking love, understanding, forgiveness or appreciation, if you let it, *Just Say Father* will strike a deep chord with you and will put you on a path toward better understanding these important relationships and realizing your goals."

—Drew Stein, CEO & Co-Founder, AuDIGENT

"All of Fred Hartley's books are profound, but *Just Say Father* may be his most important work. Every person who has been greatly used of God has come to know Him deeply. *Just Say Father* shows the path to go beyond a casual acquaintance to a stunning intimacy with God that is your spiritual birthright. Experiencing God's fatherhood solves our deepest needs."

—Bill Elliff, Founding Pastor, The Summit Church,
Little Rock AR

"*Just Say Father* is a powerful book, written to explore and expose *Father*'s heart to His children, and how we should relate to Him. The story of a father putting his hand on his baby's head and blessing him every night, and the baby expectantly awaiting this act, though not fully understanding its meaning and depth, moved me deeply. May we expectantly receive our *Father*'s blessings, trusting Him as He reparents us."

—Jamel Patterson MD MDH, President,
Ageno Foundational International, Inc.

"*Just Say Father* is a personal, emotionally touching book that challenges followers of Jesus to ponder how our *Father* in heaven desires to build us in our faith and walk. It is sprinkled with personal examples and historical anecdotes that mix current cultural figures with Puritan fathers to lead us in re-examining our understanding of "our *Father* in heaven." This is a biblically faithful call to God's people to enjoy our *Father*. I recommend this book to anyone desiring to be challenged by a fresh look at the God who loves us and is our *Father*."

—Art Nitz, PhD, Professor of Physical Therapy,
University of Kentucky

"*Just Say Father* is a masterpiece! Fred Hartley reveals the depths of his honest, insightful and challenging look, for millions of people, who need to encounter *Father*. I endorse *Just Say Father!*"

—Donn Thomas, Songwriter & Minister-At-Large

Just Say

FATHER

An Invitation to Be Re-Parented by God

FRED A. HARTLEY III

CLC PUBLICATIONS

Fort Washington, PA 19034

Just Say Father
Published by CLC Publications

U.S.A.
P.O. Box 1449, Fort Washington, PA 19034

UNITED KINGDOM
CLC International (UK)
Unit 5, Glendale Avenue, Sandycroft, Flintshire, CH5 2QP

For permission to reprint, please contact us at permissions@clcpublications.com

Printed in the United States of America

ISBN-13 (paperback): 978-1-61958-331-3
ISBN-13 (e-book): 978-1-61958-332-0

Italics in Scripture quotations are the emphasis of the author.

To Sherry—

In you I have seen
more of the Father,
and with you I have encountered
more of the Father
than with anyone else on earth.

Contents

Introduction

SOME BOOKS take months to write, some take years, and I suppose some can be written on the red-eye from JFK to LA. This book, on the other hand, has literally taken fifty years to put on paper. It was fifty years ago this month when I first called God *Father*, and He called me *son*. It has taken the better part of a lifetime to wrap my head and my heart around the reality that, in Christ, *Father* has wrapped Himself around me.

Father is profoundly personal to me. I tell you without apology that I can hardly say *Father* without a tear of appreciation. It would be utterly impossible for me to pen this book with integrity without making it personal. After all, *Father* is personal. That's the point—*Father* is personal by nature, and He wants to be personal to me, to you, to all.

The intimacy of my journey with *Father* is what actually qualifies me to be able to objectively write this book. It would be entirely inappropriate for me, or anyone, to try to depersonalize *Father*. I will certainly do my best to always remain objective, systematic, and creative as I communicate *Father*, but you need to know that the only way you can genuinely know Him is by an encounter.

You should also know that this book flows from my own prayer life. Every sentence echoes from my times with *Father*—some private *Father* times, and some corporate.

Every time I use the name *Father*, it will be italicized, and for good reason. Though we use the name frequently, it will never be used casually or meaninglessly. Hopefully the italics will not distract you, but if they do, simply imagine the italics represent a smudge on the page caused by a teardrop of gratitude. There is a tear in my spirit every time I say *Father*.

As we enter the realm of *Father*, I need all the help I can get, so in preparation for writing this book, I have read and re-read dozens of worthy *Father* books. These books form a full orchestra, each adding their own distinct sound to the symphony of *Father*. To give credit where credit is due, they are included here, and listed alphabetically by author.

John Arnott, *The Father's Blessing*[1]

John Eldridge, *Fathered by God*[2]

John Fisher, *Twelve Steps to the Recovering Pharisee*[3]

Richard Foster, *Celebration of Discipline*[4]

Richard Foster, *Prayer: Finding the Heart's True Home*[5]

Jack Frost, *Experiencing the Father's Embrace*[6]

Jack Frost, *Spiritual Slavery to Spiritual Sonship*[7]

Tim Keller, *Prodigal God*[8]

Brennan Manning, *Abba's Child*[9]

D. Martyn-Lloyd Jones, *Romans (Chapter 8:5–17) The Sons of God*[10]

Donald Miller, *To Own a Dragon*[11]

Henri Nouwen, *The Return of the Prodigal Son*[12]

John Piper, *Desiring God*[13]

John Piper, *The Pleasures of God*[14]

Thomas Smail, *The Forgotten Father*[15]

Gary Smalley and John Trent, *The Blessing*[16]

Mark Stibbe, *From Orphans to Heirs*[17]

When you want to find *Father*, there are essentially three places to look: in people, in *Father's* book, the Bible, and most accurately, in His Son. We will draw generously from all three sources, particularly from the Son. No one knows *Father* better than the Son; after all, He's been with His Dad from the beginning. If you are among those who would say, "*Father*, yes—Jesus, no," I promise to you my respect, and I would ask you for patience before you rule Him out. As we plunge into the depths of *Father*, it is only appropriate that Jesus will be our guide; He is, after all, the one who said, "No one comes to the *Father* but through me" (John 14:6).

1

Father

FATHER. NO WORD better captures the genius of God than *Father*. *Father* is His name choice, not mine nor anyone else's. You can call Him *Dad*, *Daddy*, *Papa*, *Abba*, or any number of other affectionate parental names, as long as you are talking to *Father*.

If the realm of encountering God is the ocean, then *Father* is the shallow entry point at sea level where you first get your feet wet. When you initially meet *Father*, you say something like, "*Abba*! *Daddy*!" This welcome-to-the-family interaction with *Father* is like the shallow end of the kiddy pool, or zero entry into the ocean. What I only recently realized is that *Father* is also the Mariana Trench. The deepest place you can go on the ocean floor is the Mariana Trench, and the deepest place you will ever go with God is *Father*. No matter where you are on the spiritual growth chart—whether you are a newborn infant or a maturing adult—*Father* is waiting for you. He is the secure footing beneath you, and simultaneously calling you to go deeper.

Father is the solitary name that captures both the complexity and the simplicity of God. It is the one name that is equally understood by both the preschooler and the Rhodes scholar, by the crackhead and the cleric, by the novice and the expert alike. *Father* offers every breathing person on earth equal footing before Almighty God. No two people relate to God in the same exact way because no two people are identical. As of today, there are 7,846,000,000 people living on earth, and there echoes in the pit of my soul, your soul, and the belly of every other soul on earth, a longing for *Father*.

> **THERE IS NO MORE NOBLE QUEST ON EARTH THAN THE QUEST TO KNOW *FATHER*.**

Father not only gave you your own fingerprint, He gave you a unique personhood, identity, and calling, and your relationship with Him will also be entirely your own. Humanity is not longing for seven billion different daddies—not even seven. While every person's journey to discover *Father* is completely unique, each one of us longs for one *Dad*—we long for *Father*.

There is no more noble quest on earth than the quest to know *Father*. Every other pursuit that drives us—some which drive us to greatness, and some to insanity—are all an effort to discover what is only found in *Father*.

Your *Father* journey is not simply the adventure of a lifetime—it will last for eternity. For the next gazillion years, you will still be exploring the invigoratingly inexhaustible depths of *Father*. While sailors do their best to stay above the surface of the water, the oceanographer has one objective—to explore the gold mine of secrets beneath the surface. Oceanographers make a living going deep, and so do *Father*-seekers. Fortunately, you don't need to be a research scientist to know Him; He wants to help you feel secure in the shallows, as well as to assist you as you explore His jaw-dropping depths.

Your pursuit of *Father*, as you will discover, is also your pursuit of self. Only *Father* can help you truly be yourself because He fully accepts you and loves you unconditionally. He alone can help you remove your masks—the masks that hide your insecurities and enable you to pose, pretend and fake it. He also helps you remove your labels—labels like Jew, Catholic, Protestant, Muslim, intellectual, scholar, jock, lesbian, gay, straight, OCD, bi-polar, addict, alcoholic, druggie, prostitute; or less flattering labels like nerd, geek, dysfunctional, loser, bed-wetter, ugly, ignoramus, irreverent, worthless, loser, trash.

All your labels, stickers, and tattoos try to define you, and yet, even when they are accurate, the result of all of them is the same—they devalue you. *Father* devalues no one. Labels make you smaller than you are. Even labels like white, African-American, Latino, Asian, while potentially accurate, are incomplete—you are more than your ethnicity.

Low self-esteem is the curse of our species; *Father* is the cure. For this reason, He sees past your labels. He sees you for who you are, and He wants to call you to greatness. He wants to call you *child*, and He wants to call you *Mine*. He wants you to call him *Father*.

Father Rocks

In case you think this father-thing is just a Bible-thing, it's not. Rock music is full of this father-thing because as raw, angry, and violent as rock music can be, it is nevertheless real, and so is *Father*. Justin Bieber wrote a piano ballad "Where Are You Now" in which he asks hard questions as he describes his complex relationship with his dad. Before the end of the song, he cries out words that struck a chord in millions of hearts in which he invites his dad back into his life.[1]

Christina Aguilera wrote a raw song, "Hurt," from the depth of her grief as she tried to process the loss of her dad and their fiery relationship. "It ended up being this beautiful song about my dad," she explained, "and the pain that I'm going through, and the guilt and regret for not being more present with him."[2]

Bono of U2 described his dad as, "A tough old boot of a guy." In 2002, at his dad's funeral, he sang the tribute song he had written, "Tough." The song was re-mixed in 2004 in his album, *How to Dismantle an Atomic Bomb* with the penetrating observation that he sees his dad's reflection whenever he looks in the mirror.[3]

Few musicians have put so much raw emotion from their own private lives into their music as Eric Clapton. In his autobiography *I Tried*, he shares at length the story behind his gut-wrenching song, "My Father's Eyes," describing what felt like a sucker-punch when he learned his "sister" with whom he grew up was actually his "mom," and his "mom" was actually his grandma.[4]

These are only a few among the hundreds of examples of this father-thing found in rock music. The reason rock music is so full of this father-thing is because life is so full of it. These father-songs have sold millions of copies, not simply because fans identify with father-wounds from their biological dads, but because people long for a relationship with a more transcendent *Dad*. While having some degree of a healthy relationship with dad is a universal longing, this soul-cry for *Father* runs even deeper. *Father* is the common denominator of our humanity. It is no accident that *Father* God programmed this father-thing inside our DNA. In essence, this father-thing is God's mark of ownership in every one of us.

Thomas Wolfe was one of the great literary geniuses in American history. William Faulkner even called Wolfe's second novel the best prose of his generation. Wolfe's writing was so honest, reflective, and vulnerable that it caused an outrage among the people in his hometown, many of whom thought his novel was overly critical and indiscreet. In response to the outrage, Wolfe published *The Story of a Novel*, essentially a book about writing a book. It was based on a lecture he had given shortly after completing his soul-searching novel. In it he points out a central flaw in our DNA:

> The deepest search in life, it seemed to me, the thing that in one way or another was central to all living was man's search to find a father, not merely the father of his flesh, not merely the lost father of his youth, but the image of a strength and wisdom external to his need and superior to his hunger, to which the belief and power of his own life could be united.[5]

In our society, fatherlessness runs deep, and father-wounds are almost as common as bellybuttons—but they don't heal as fast as physical wounds, and they often get infected. One-third of the children in the United States are living in a home without their biological dad, and the global average is even higher. But fatherlessness only accounts for a thin slice of father-wounds. Parental abuse comes in many shapes and sizes. It is utterly tragic to realize that your dad—the one person who, of all people, should love and bless you—can become the source of your greatest pain.

Re-parenting

My *Father* journey began fifty years ago today—yes, today of all things. When He first invited me to just say *Father*, I had no idea what I was in for, but I knew He was real and my encounter with Him was authentic. I came alive inside and almost immediately felt whole. His presence became the air I breathe; reading His book, the Bible, became food for my soul, and my *Father*-time became the highlight of my day.

But don't get me wrong—my *Father* journey, while authentic, has not always been smooth sailing. *Father* recently gave me a stiff warning—more like a stinging rebuke: "Fred, never treat your *Father*-time as common," He said. "Never allow what you teach on prayer to become mechanical or routine. No matter how often you lead my people to encounter Me, it must never get old or cold."

I instantly knew it was *Father*. His words cut my heart like a filleting knife. I instantly knew I was both loved and in trouble. You see, in 1997, I started a small ministry in Atlanta that has since become a global movement called the College of Prayer. As of today, we have 348,195 campuses, more than one million Revival Prayer Groups, and 16,782,318 students in 136 nations of the world, and within the next year, we are on track to serve the church in every nation on earth. But in that moment, I instantly knew my heart had grown cold, my prayers had gotten old, and my teaching had become stale. *Father* loved me too much to allow me to succeed professionally, while shriveling up like a dead lizard on a hot sidewalk personally.

What happened next changed my life.

I immediately cried out, "Oh *Father*, I am a mess. I need help!" Then I asked, "But how, Lord—how can my old heart become young and alive again?" As clearly as I have ever heard his voice, *Father* spoke four words that I had never before heard. These four words would forever change my life: "Let Me re-parent you," *Father* said. Hmmm. He said them a second, and then third time: "Let Me re-parent you." I replayed them in my mind. Over and over again, repeating them slowly, as if sucking a verbal lollipop—Let Me re-parent you. They tasted fresh, alive—and the more I said them, the more effervescent and explosive they became.

> ## IN THE RADIANT FACE OF *FATHER*, I WAS REDUCED TO A CHILD.

Within moments, it was as though *Father* barged into my room, took me by the hand as the big-shot president of the College of Prayer, and escorted me back to preschool. The degrees on my wall and the accomplishments in my résumé seemed to evaporate into insignificance. In the radiant face of *Father*, I was reduced to a child.

It was delightful! I had always thought that brand-new followers related to Him as *Father*, but not me. Somehow my pride and arrogance made me feel superior, independent, and self-sufficient, as if I didn't require daily interaction with *Abba*, but this day *Father's* words broke me. I had never heard these four words before—*let Me re-parent you*—but the more I rolled them around my tongue, the more I liked the taste. They even seemed vaguely and distantly familiar, and the more I savored them, the more they tasted like my mother's breast milk and less like a lollipop—far more nutritious than a ball of candy on the end of a stick. This became a defining moment in my life. These four words have led me on the most revolutionary, healing journey of my life. I can tell you today, *Father* is re-parenting me, and I know it's only the beginning.

These four words—*let Me re-parent you*—have both refreshed me and wrecked me. They have both renewed me and ruined me, satisfied me and spanked me. I never want to spend another day without *Father* nor another day without His re-parenting. They have certainly rejuvenated my fifty-year-old prayer life and revolutionized my thinking. This book flows from a deep well that is still being dug in my soul by these four words. They are so profoundly personal to me that until recently I genuinely thought I was the only one on earth to receive the invitation to be re-parented.

I was thrilled to learn that my friend John Eldridge is also being re-parented: "God wants to father us. The truth is, he has been fathering us for a long time—we just haven't had the eyes to see it. He wants to father us much more intimately, but we have to be in the right posture to receive it."[6] Creative writer Donald Miller admits that he, too, is being re-parented: "I said this out loud: I want God to father me."[7]

When I read Eldridge's and Miller's words, I felt like I found a couple of soulmates—at least I was no longer the only guy on earth being re-parented. Miller went on to explain, "I liked the fact Jesus said we could call God Father. And even though I had read that passage [of the Lord's Prayer] many times before, in this new light it felt revolutionary."[8] Revolutionary indeed, and you will discover just how radical and revolutionary it is.

Reflections

As you look at *Father*, you can see your own reflection because you are fashioned in His likeness. In the delightful Disney classic, *The Lion King*, the lead lion Simba faced a world-class identity crisis. Because of personal guilt and a father-wound, he ran away from his family and lost himself in an alternate jungle. At a pivotal moment in the film, little Simba, without being self-aware, and seemingly overnight, becomes a mature male lion. As he goes to the local watering hole for a casual drink, this jungle scene becomes one of the greatest identity discovery moments in film history. Leaning over the water, Simba is startled to see a mature lion looking up at him. His reflection looks eerily like his deceased father, Mufasa. Simba tries to deny it: "That's not my father. That's just my reflection," he sighs. But his playful monkey friend, Rafiki, doesn't let him off so easily. To reinforce the gravity of the moment, "No, look harder," Rafiki says as he swats the water with a stick and the ripples change the reflection to more clearly resemble Mufasa. Rafiki insists, "You see, he lives in you." Then in the deep, gravelly, booming voice of none other than James Earl Jones, Mufasa speaks.

Mufasa: "Simba, have you forgotten me?"

Simba: "No. How could I?"

This is where the conversation strikes gold. The question on the table is, how could I forget my father? Now listen to the profound wisdom Mufasa gives his son:

Mufasa: "You have forgotten who you are, and so forgotten me. Look inside yourself, Simba. You are more than what you have become."

Simba: "How could I go back? I am not who I used to be."

Mufasa: "Remember who you are. You are my son, and the one true king. Remember who you are."[9]

While I hesitate to admit it, *The Lion King* packs more *Father* wisdom into a one-hour fifty-eight-minute film than most preachers do in a lifetime of sermons. Notice the connection between forgetting his father and losing himself. Notice who it is who calls forth the best in Simba, and who reminds him, "You are more than what you have become." Simba wanted to avoid the guilt and shame of returning home, but there was one who could convince him of his identity—his dad. Mufasa was the one to call out his son's identity, nobility, and destiny, and *Father* is the one to call out yours. This becomes the self-discovery turning point not only for Simba, but for everyone in his circle of influence.

It's not surprising that *The Lion King* broke every box office record and established the Mouse House as far and away the most powerful animated film studio in the industry. Originally it grossed $968 million in 1994, which converts to about $1.676 billion in 2019 money. The reason for its blockbuster success is obviously not because people like animated lions, but because people long for identity—they long for *Father*.

Allow me to tell you some things about yourself.

- You are created with a capacity to know *Father*.

- Your quest for your identity is inseparably linked to your hunt for *Father*.

- You will find yourself when you find *Father*.

- Your fulfillment in life depends on your relationship with *Father*.

- The depth of your soul and your personal maturity depends on your intimacy with *Father*.

If any of these statements sound like a stretch, they will come into clearer focus as we journey together in the process that follows. You may have to watch your waistline to impress people, but you don't need to impress *Father*. He does not care if you have six-pack abs and a rock-hard butt. In fact, all the games you and I play to impress people are probably projecting a false self, and I promise you, your false self is unknown to God. It is impossible for God to know your false self because, by definition, your false self does not exist.

Now let me tell you a few things about *Father*.

- *Father* knows you inside and out—every eyebrow hair, every wart and freckle, every heartache and aspiration.

- *Father* loves you unconditionally—there is nothing you can do to make Him love you more, and there is nothing you can do to make Him love you less.

- *Father* sent His Son into our human orphanage for one purpose—to show you how much he loves you and to pay for your adoption.

- *Father* knows you by heart and He wants you to know Him by heart.

Let me clarify—this book is not so much about your dad as it is about your *Dad*. As a life-long student of both dads and *Dad*, I have observed an unusual pattern: a good dad does not guarantee you a relationship with *Dad*, nor does a bad dad in any way prevent you from a relationship with *Dad*. I have friends with great dads who have allowed their father to become such an iconic role model that they never saw the need nor had the desire to develop a relationship with *Father*; and I have friends with abusive or absent fathers who became so bitter and resentful that they projected their hatred on *Father*. I also have friends whose dads are rock-stars and, at least partially because of the godly example of their dads, were motivated to pursue *Father*; and still others whose dads were abusive addicts, yet my friends longed for a healthy father and healing from their father-wounds and went on to discover *Father*.

When my own dad died, I was angry at *Father*. Following his open-heart surgery, his doctor told me, "He's doing fine; we've never lost a patient in his condition, and we won't lose him." And then he died. It took me eight years to process his loss before I was able to encounter *Dad* on a level He always wanted.

THERE IS NO FATHER-WOUND THAT *FATHER* CANNOT HEAL.

I've learned that there is no perfect dad, but there is a perfect *Dad*. There is not a good or even a rock-star dad who is ever good enough to replace *Father*. There is no rotten dad whom *Dad* cannot redeem, there is no father-wound that *Father* cannot heal, and there is no need for dad that *Dad* cannot meet. I guess the only pattern I discovered in my life-long, clinical study is there is no pattern—no predictable pattern—but there is a redeeming *Father* who is here for you today.

The coolest part of *Father* is that no one has a leg up on anybody else. Regardless of how good (or not so good) your biological dad may have been, it does not necessarily increase or decrease your capacity to know *Father*. Your biological dad may have been a world-class father, and while that is a blessing, it does not necessarily give you an advantage at gaining greater intimacy with *Father*. Or, to the other end of the father spectrum, your dad may have been a loser—abusive, addictive, mean-spirited, angry, or absent—and you may have father-wounds that still require healing, but you need to know that you are not disqualified—you have just as much access to the healing affection of *Father* as anyone else. In fact, as you will discover, in some ways you have more. The coolest part of *Father* is that He is ready, willing and able to redeem you, and He is ready to start today. No one is in a better place to start a relationship with *Father* than you are in right now. If you have never in your life read a Christian book, or if your shelves are full of them, the good news is, God wants to re-parent you, and He wants to start now.

One disclaimer: *Father* is not a genie in a bottle who pops out and promises your first three wishes. He is not some mantra you can chant, nor a magic word like hocus pocus, nor a get-out-of-jail-free Monopoly card. He is not the pot of gold at the end of a rainbow, or someone who takes you to Disney World every day. *Just Say Father* does not hand you the skeleton key to open all the God-doors in your life, nor will it instantly remove all heartaches and disappointments. And you don't need *Father for Dummies*. Some knock-off, two-bit, hallucinogenic religious hucksters may be peddling a distorted view of *Father*, but not here. Don't allow anyone to devalue the name of ultimate worth, of such profound meaning, of such unspeakable treasure. The name *Father* is profoundly personal and entirely affectionate that you don't dare want to dumb Him down.

Abba

In your home, the kids may call their dad by any number of affectionate and appropriate names: daddy, pops, dad, father. I pastor a church in metro Atlanta with members who were born in over 70 different nations of the world, and it amazes me how many of their little children call their dad *abba*. Jesus grew up in a culture where children commonly called their dad abba. This makes perfect sense. What does not make perfect sense is that God invites you and me to

use this endearing, affectionate, profoundly intimate name
when we talk to Him—*Abba*. *Father's* book says, "You have
received the Spirit of adoption as sons, by whom we cry,
'*Abba! Father!*'" (Romans 8:15). Notice it does not say, by
whom we cried, as if we only say *Abba, Father,* the moment
we are first introduced to Him. It says, by whom we cry,
which means *Abba* is an ongoing part of our conversation
with Him regardless of how old we are.

Abba is like *dada* or *papa*, yet even simpler to say. It is
the simplest two syllable word you will ever speak. If you
simply tighten your vocal cords while breathing out, you say
aaaaahhh. If you simply close your lips once while breathing
out, you say aaaaahhh-baaa or *Abba*. It's simple, childlike and
basic. Not surprisingly, this is precisely the word the Holy
Spirit helps you say when he teaches you to pray.

I want to ask you to consider praying a little prayer. The
entire prayer is only six words. It is so short, it may at first
sound trite or even harmless, but it's not. *Father* likes short
prayers; most of us do too. Whether you realize it today or
not, these six words are the due north on the compass inside
of your chest, and they will take you on the greatest journey
of your life—your journey home. I will give you the opportunity to pray this small prayer at the end of each chapter,
and hopefully, it will become your prayer for the rest of your
life. As one who has prayed it virtually every day for several
years, I can tell you, it has the power to change you from the
inside out.

Father, re-parent me in Jesus' name.

2

Father's Heart

FATHER HAS A heart. The reason you have one is because He does.

Father's heart is His essence—full of virtue, dignity, royalty, nobility, and full of joy, adventure, affection, and spontaneity. *Father's* heart is healthy, humble, and *Father's* heart is whole. Unlike my heart and yours, *Father's* heart is undamaged; in fact, fortunately for you and me, it is not only undamaged, it is undamageable. *Father* never struggles with identity issues.

He never stays up at night wondering who He is, and He never wakes up in the morning questioning His life-purpose. Though He has been around for a long, long time, you never need to worry about Him getting dementia, Alzheimer's, or senility. If you can imagine, He doesn't even require sleep, so He doesn't miss a thing. His heart is pure. Clean. Good. True. Just. Kind. Compassionate. Understanding. Forgiving. Child-like. And best of all, *Father's* heart is radically in love with you. *Father*-thinker Richard Foster said it this way:

> His heart is the most sensitive and tender of all. No act goes unnoticed, no matter how insignificant or small. A cup of cold water is enough to put tears in the eyes of God. Like a

29

proud mother who receives a wilted bouquet of dandelions
from her child so God celebrates our feeble expressions of
gratitude.[1]

Inside *Father's* heart is where you first existed. I obviously
don't mean that biologically you were somehow part of a
ginormous embryonic mass inside the being of God, like the
clones in Star Wars, but you were in His thoughts, purposes,
and plan. You were conceived initially and conceptually inside *Father* before you were conceived inside your mother. He
oversaw the nine months of your gestation, as well as your
birthing process, but His involvement runs much deeper than
just being a silent observer. Listen to one man's description of
Father's intimate interaction during his prenatal days:

> For you formed my inward parts;
>   you knitted me together in my mother's womb.
> I praise you, for I am fearfully and wonderfully made.
> Wonderful are your works;
>   my soul knows it very well.
> My frame was not hidden from you,
> when I was being made in secret,
>   intricately woven in the depths of the earth.
> Your eyes saw my unformed substance;
> in your book were written, every one of them,
>   the days that were formed for me,
>   when as yet there was none of them.
>
>   Ps. 139:13–16

Whether you realize it or not, you have been in *Father's* heart
long before your birth. For this reason, you will never find
yourself until you find yourself in *Father*, and the heart-cry
for your identity is actually a haunting cry from the depth of
your soul for *Father*.

Your Heart

Somewhere down near the pit of your stomach, underneath your labels, stickers, and tattoos, is your heart. Your heart is the essence of who you are—your core. While your heart feels emotion, your heart is much deeper than mere feelings. Your heart stores your uniqueness, personality, humor, and pizzazz, but it is still deeper than even your personality. Your heart is the seat of your affections, aspirations, motivations. Decision-making, risk-taking, and feats of greatness all start in your heart. Your heart is your identity.

> **WHATEVER RULES YOUR AFFECTIONS, RULES YOUR HEART; AND WHATEVER RULES YOUR HEART, RULES YOUR LIFE.**

Your heart is the courtroom where your values are shaped. Regardless of how religious or irreligious you may be, your heart is the throne room where you continually engage in worship. Whatever rules your affections, rules your heart; and whatever rules your heart, rules your life.

Most significantly, it's here, inside your heart, where you discover *Father*. It is not surprising the Bible warns, "Keep your heart with all vigilance, for from it flow the springs of life" (Prov. 4:23).

When you read the term "*Father*'s heart," you need to understand that you are included—the term does not simply refer to Him; it refers to you. The heart of *Father* that longs for you reflects the heart in you that longs, even subliminally, for Him. Both hearts—yours and His—are connected, and both hearts find fulfilment, identity, and life-purpose in each other. *Father* God fiercely longs for your heart, and whether you know it or not, your heart deep down desperately longs for Him.

It may be helpful to compare and contrast your heart and His.

Your Heart	*Father's Heart*
Made in His likeness	Himself
Broken/Damaged	Whole
Impure	Pure
Needing identity	Source of identity
Looking for Him	Looking for you

Cardio

Our generation knows better than any other in history that cardio exercise is good for our health. The problem is, we only focus on the physical heart. You and I were born with two hearts—one that is physical and one that is metaphysical; one that keeps you alive and one that makes your life worth living; one that pumps blood and the other that pumps love; one is your heart and the other we could perhaps more appropriately call your heart of hearts. Both are essential to a healthy life, and yet, because they are both invisible to the eye, they both tend to be neglected. The *Father*-philosopher Augustine gives a profound insight in his tour de force *Confessions*: "You have made us for yourself, O Lord, and our heart is restless until it rests in you."[2]

To call *Father* a cardiologist is an understatement. He is not just one good doctor among many; he is the Surgeon General—the stand-alone expert on all things heart. He not only created it, restores it, and fulfills it, He promises to completely replace it. *Father* says to you, "I will give you a new heart, and a new spirit I will put within you. And I will remove the heart of stone from your flesh and give you a heart of flesh" (Ezek. 36:26).

Henry Scougal wrote an obscure book in 1677, *The Life of God and the Soul of Man*. Though only twenty-seven years old at the time, he makes a profound heart-insight: "The worth and excellency of a soul is to be measured by the object of its love."[3] Scougal put his finger on something imbedded deep inside our humanity that seeks an object to love. Scougal went on to explain: "He who loveth mean and sordid things doth thereby become base and vile; but a noble and well-placed affection doth advance and improve the spirit unto a conformity with the perfections which it loves."[4]

Scougal exposed the essential nature of the heart which motivated John Piper to write *The Pleasure of God*. Heart is where we love—not the mushy-gushy, sentimental, warm-fuzzy puppy love, but the all-encompassing, self-sacrificing, self-discovering, worth-dying-for love. This is the pearl-of-great-price, climb-any-mountain, cross-any-ocean, conquer-any-obstacles, compelling type of love. To word it differently, heart is where we worship what we ultimately love. It's this full-throttle, all-in type worship that determines your worth, purpose, and life-calling. What you love and passionately pursue to this extent is what you worship in your heart of hearts.

Knowing by Heart

One of the great tragedies of our day is that the heart is dumbed down by both the materialist and the mystic alike. The former sees the heart as an overworked muscle with an impeccable sense of timing, while the latter regards it as a sort of ethereal jewel box inside your soul where you put sentimental trinkets inside a lace doily with a splash of lavender potpourri. Both perspectives miss the point. The heart is much more than a blood pump, and it is certainly more than a pouch for warm memories and potpourri. Your heart is what drives you to greatness—it is where dreams, goals, aspirations take flight. Your heart is what separates you from the almost 8 billion other people on earth, and most importantly, as we have said, your heart is where you know *Father*.

It may be easier to understand what it means to know *Father* by hearing from people throughout history who knew Him by heart.

Mother Teresa was one of the most passionate *Father*-lovers who ever lived. In more ways than one, she wrote the book on loving *Father*. She summarized her life mission in the title of her book, *Where There is Love, There is God*. On one occasion she was asked the straightforward question, "Who is God?" and she simply replied, "God is love."[5] Bullseye.

I have often wondered what motivated a single woman to invest her life caring for the most marginalized, poorest of the poor, helpless, hopeless orphans on earth. The answer is obvious—*Father*. She lived and breathed *Father*. She said, "What blood is to the body, prayer is to the soul." She was such a healthy, loving soul, she said, "We have been created for greater things, to love and to be loved." When asked who is God, she responded, "God is love and He loves you, and we are precious to Him. He calls us by our name. We belong to Him. He has created us in His image for greater things. God is love, God is joy, God is life, God is truth."[6]

Harriet Tubman, known as the woman who freed the slaves, gave all credit for her success to *Father*: "When I found I had crossed that line, I looked at my hands to see if I was the same person. There was such a glory over everything; the sun came like gold through trees, and over the fields, and I felt like I was in heaven."[7] With every slave she led to freedom, she encountered *Father's* love.

Fanny Crosby, though blind from infancy, had an indomitable spirit and overcame her limitations. Known and loved as the queen of gospel songwriters, she authored more than 8,000 songs and more than 1,000 poems. Her most frequent theme was the love of *Father*.

> God is love! His Word proclaims it,
>   Day by day he proves
> Heaven 'n earth with joy are telling,
>   ever telling God is love.

Three women—Mother Teresa, Harriet Tubman, and Fanny Crosby—three different ethnicities, three different continents, three different stories; yet they all discovered their life-calling, and accomplished great things, because they each knew *Father*.

Not surprisingly, the Bible contains its own archive of legendary *Father*-lovers. David, the king, was known as a man after God's own heart[8] who wrote love songs to *Father*: "Because your steadfast love is better than life, my lips will praise you" (Ps. 63:3). Paul, the apostle, wrote, "The love of Christ controls us" (2 Cor. 5:14), and, "Nothing . . . will be able to separate us from the love of God in Christ Jesus our Lord" (Rom. 8:38–39). Jude, the half-brother of Jesus, exhorted us, "Keep yourselves in the love of God" (Jude 1:21).

Perhaps no one in history was captured by the love of *Father* quite as thoroughly as the apostle John. He was the only Bible author to write the words, "God is love," and he wrote them twice.[9] He was the only apostle to record the words of Jesus exhorting his successors to "love one another," and did so four times.[10] He is the only Gospel writer to record Jesus asking his lead disciple the probing question, "Peter, do you love me?," and he asked it three times.[11] He is the one who records Jesus using the name *Father*, referring to or addressing God, no less than 123 times—more than all the other Gospel writers put together.

It was only John who captures the late-night conversation between Jesus and Nicodemus, when Jesus offered the greatest news to our orphaned humanity, "You must be born again" (John 3:7).

John wrote profoundly about *Father* because he was in love with *Father*. For him, *Father* was not a religious formula, and love was more than a mere emotional attraction—it was the greatest force on earth. Perhaps the most vivid moment recorded from John's life was when he rested his head on Jesus' chest.[12] Think about it: John put his head next to Jesus' heart.

While this is only a snapshot moment in time, it reflects a deeper reality: what was inside Jesus' heart is what changed John's heart. I wonder, What would happen if you and I would rest our head against Jesus' heart and listen closely? It is no wonder John described himself as "the disciple Jesus loved" (John 21:20). I want to follow John's example—I want to lay my head near Jesus' heart and become the disciple whom Jesus loved. History tells us that John was the youngest of Jesus' disciples, outliving all the others, living into his nineties, and his long life gave him the luxury of more years on earth to get to know *Father*.

Password

We use passwords to protect things of value. As our digital footprint grows, passwords are easily forgotten. We think,

Is it my birthday? My anniversary? My address? The initials of my favorite football team? You may not realize it, but your heart is also password protected, and for good reason: You don't want just anyone walking into your heart of hearts—your inner self—to steal your worth, your dignity, or your personhood.

> ## FATHER WANTS TO CONNECT WITH YOU HEART-TO-HEART.

Finding your heart password can be challenging. You try to enter the obvious—nationality, family tree, address, birthday, parent's names, bank account, social security number—but all these passwords fail to work. They will never unlock your heart because they are beneath you—they are too small. Anything beneath you is never the key to unlock the space within yourself that is bigger than you are. You need a password that is bigger than you—bigger than your life, your spouse, your job, your parents, your portfolio—bigger than your dreams and your wildest imagination. *Father* not only wants you to know you have a password to your heart; He wants you to know that He is the password.

Father wants to connect with you heart-to-heart. He knows you better than you know yourself, and He knows your heart password. He is waiting for you to invite Him to access your heart, and re-parent you. You have been in His heart long before your heart started beating, and He wants you to know Him. Knowing *Father* is deeper than knowing about Him, because when you know Him, you learn to trust Him.

If you are feeling it, pray with me now:

Father, re-parent me in Jesus' name.

3

Father's Hurt

DISCOVERING *FATHER*'S hurt is the way to understand *Father*'s heart. His hurt links Him to your broken humanity, and His hurt makes Him accessible to you 24/7. In reality, you will never know *Father* until you know His hurt.

It may surprise you to learn that *Father* hurts, or that He has feelings of any kind. When you think of God, you may see Him as aloof, distant, impersonal, untouched and untouchable. He may seem to you more like the impersonal Force in Star Wars and less like *Father*. You may wonder, How can He hurt? How can He even feel what we feel? I thought He was invincible and untouchable. Doesn't He have bigger things to deal with than me and my mess?

Pain is so much a part of our world, that if *Father* is distanced from pain, if He has no feelings, nor the capacity to experience pain, He would be irrelevant. If *Father* cannot relate to the heartache of a middle-school boy facing his parents' divorce, or understand the plight of an inner-city girl whose boyfriend demands she get an abortion, or feel with parents who have lost their first-born child to cancer, or the foster child who lost their only parent to COVID, what good is He?

Hate to hurt feelings.

If *Father* has no mechanism of which to register pain, no way to calibrate suffering, or means to compare one pain level against another, or if pain to Him is nothing more than a theory, then He would certainly be out of touch, and useless to me and you. If this cold, uncaring, unphased image of God is the picture you have of Him, you are in for a pleasant surprise.

Father-Wounds

Father-wounds are some of the deepest wounds on the planet, and they are caused by dads. When John Lennon was a child, his father left, and his mother put him in the care of his aunt. Following the demise of the Beatles, he wrote the song, Mother, that served as a release valve for his pent-up-grief. In it he gave a few jabs at his father, saying that he didn't leave his dad, but his father left him; he needed his father, but his father didn't need him.[1] That pretty well sums up the feeling of father-wounds. Dads who are angry, cruel, abusive, or simply absent can injure or even cripple us. Tragic.

Father-wounds have been the basis of countless blockbuster Hollywood movies. Abandonment runs deep in Hollywood films because abandonment runs deep in our human story. Every movie from *Tron*, to *Toy Story*, to *Karate Kid*, to *Batman Returns*, to *The Curious Case of Benjamin Button* is full of the cry of abandonment. In the movie *E.T. the Extra-Terrestrial*, ten-year-old Elliot discovers this endearing alien character who held up his glowing finger and said in a synthesized voice, "E.T. phone home!" The only character in the film who felt every bit as lonely and out of place as E.T. was Elliot himself. When Elliot lashes out at the dinner table over the hurt of his father's betrayal, he was not only expressing his father-wound, but the father-wound of millions of viewers. It is not surprising that more people gathered at that time to watch that film than any film in history.

Father-wounds reached epic proportion in *Star Wars Episode V: The Empire Strikes Back*. If there is one scene that stands out in all the Star Wars movies, it's this one. In one of the classic light-saber battles, Darth Vader and young Luke Skywalker climb precariously toward the end of a skinny walkway. "There is no escape! Don't make me destroy you," Vader insists. Angry Skywalker yells, "I'll never join you!" The conversation between Vader and Skywalker escalates until Vader drops the bomb: "No. I am your father!" At this point in the film, Skywalker erupts with a blood-curdling scream that still echoes through the galaxies: "NOOOOOOOOOOOOO!!!"

Rock music and Hollywood movies are not simply talking about absentee dads, father-wounds, and the cultural phenomenon of fatherlessness in our society; they point us to a deeper need. While physical orphans have needs that are real and relevant, all of us feel the soul-pain of being spiritual orphans. The heart of *Father*'s hurt are father-wounds.

Father of Compassion

Father is full of compassion. Of all *Father*'s virtues, compassion is one in which He overflows. His book, the Bible, tells us not once, but five times, He is full of compassion.[2] Perhaps more than any other virtue, as essential as all His virtues are, compassion is what tells you that *Father* feels with you. When you are in a miserable spot, whether because of your own stupidity, or someone else's, *Father* knows, He feels, and He hurts. He is affected by your pain. *Father*'s heart hurts most over your heart's lostness and His compassion is what moves Him to action. *Father's* compassion gives me hope; it gives you hope too.

The song book of the Bible captures a creative lyric that paints an accurate picture of *Father's* compassion: "As a father shows compassion [*racham*] to his children, so the LORD shows compassion to those who fear him" (Ps. 103:13). *Racham* is the Hebrew word translated compassion, and it carries imagery of a hand gently touching or tenderly fondling. This image vividly paints an outward picture of the inner heart of *Father*—He gently touches your wounds with His healing hand.

> ## YOU WILL NEVER UNDERSTAND FATHER'S HEART UNTIL YOU UNDERSTAND HIS HURT.

Father Hurts

Pain is as much a part of your humanity as your skin, and *Father*, who is linked to your humanity, is linked to your pain. Good dads hurt when their kids hurt, and every hurt in us hurts *Father*. From the moment you fought your way through your mother's birth canal and the doctor's firm, cold hand slapped your bare-naked butt to make you cry your first breath, pain is as much a part of life as breath—and *Father* feels it all. As we said, you will never understand *Father's* heart until you understand His hurt. Every hurt in us not only hurts *Father*, but as we will discover, it is personally connected to *Father*.

To better understand *Father's* heart, I want to introduce you to Fred Pepperman. Fred and his wife Julie lived in Tennessee with their four daughters: Grace, 16; Olivia, 20; Mellory, 22; and Kathryn, 24. As they approached their wedding anniversary, they decided to bring their four daughters with them to Florida's Gulf Coast near Panama City, Florida, where they honeymooned twenty-eight years earlier. On Sunday, July 14, 2019, they went to enjoy the sun and surf. Fred had just settled into his beach chair when his youngest daughter, sixteen-year-old Grace, began to desperately scream for help. A fierce riptide that was previously unnoticed began to drag her out to sea. Fred and Julie immediately jumped up and ran toward the water, but their daughters Olivia and Kathryn, who were closer to the water, got there first. They too got caught in the current, and now all three girls were screaming for help. Fred got to Kathryn and Grace and pushed them out of the current, as by-standers from the beach brought them to safety.

Olivia was still in desperate trouble, and Fred instantly knew what needed to be done. He turned, put his head down, and swam as fast as he could paddle. Olivia cried, "Daddy, help me!" As he grabbed his daughter, he spoke his final words, "I got you."[3] Struggling with all the energy he had, he fought against the relentless riptide, and with every gasping breath, thrust his precious daughter toward shore. By now people had formed a human chain and were able to grab Olivia and safely pulled her to the beach.

Fred, however, was exhausted. His strength was drained. He had spent himself fighting to save his daughters, and one last time the current dragged him under.

When they pulled his body out of the Gulf minutes later, they laid him on the sand, limp and lifeless. Julie and their four daughters gathered around him sobbing, praying, administering CPR, stroking his arms and legs, crying out, "Daddy! Please don't go!" But it was too late. Fred was gone. He was taken to the nearby hospital where he was pronounced dead.

The next day his wife posted an honorable tribute on her Facebook page:

> Thank you to everyone for your thoughts and prayers. Around 12:30 on July 14, 2019, Fred Pepperman gave his life to save his family. If it wasn't for his efforts, Grace and Olivia definitely would have been lost and Kathryn and myself probably would have been lost. He was amazing, selfless, tireless, and committed to making sure we were all out of the water. Once we were safe, he was simply too exhausted to worry about himself. His body was worn out. Fred lived his life being kind to everyone and sharing his big heart. I was blessed that God placed him in my life at 16 and allowed me to have him for 32 years. Next Friday, the 26th would have been our 28th wedding anniversary. He was my love and a wonderful father to our children. You did good, Freddie. Our girls are safe. You saved your family. You are a good man, through and through. We love you and our hearts are breaking![4]

The following Sunday, before the family drove back to their home in Tennessee, Julie gathered her daughters and a few friends and family on the beach for a small, solemn memorial. It was a time full of honor, sorrow, tears and tributes where Julie made several observations about Fred: "He died a hero, saving his daughters lives in his favorite place in the world. We were less than a mile from where we celebrated our marriage twenty-eight years ago. We had a night with the whole family together and we have family around us to help us and support us."[5] She added, "Fred died doing exactly what a dad is supposed to do."[6] Julie said, "Everyone thought Fred would want boys, but I think he really wanted girls. Once we had our first daughter, he was thrilled to welcome three more. They all had him wrapped around their fingers."[7] Fred had coached their softball teams, taught them to fish, and never missed a school event. Then Julie added, "If God told Fred that morning he was going to go, I don't think he would have picked a different way."[8] The last thing this model-dad said was what every child wants to hear from their dad: "I got you."

There are a thousand father virtues that drip from this sacred story: a marriage worth celebrating after twenty-eight years; parents who invite their adult-children on their anniversary get-away; kids who want to go; a reunion in the same location where the magic began; a mother who helped her four daughters see a dad who died saving those he loved most; the goodness of God even in the face of extreme sorrow and loss. I have read and reread this story a dozen times. If someone could bottle the dignity of this dad, you could heal the ills of most cities.

But the real story within the story is *Father*. This dad bears a striking resemblance to *Dad*. Fred Pepperman was a special guy who stands among a very small group of dads. Good dads feel and identify with the needs of their children. Fred Pepperman illustrates the essence of both *Father*'s heart and *Father*'s hurt. When Fred heard the desperate scream, he felt her anguish, he felt the unthinkable prospect of his daughter drowning, and he had compassion that caused him to lunge from his beach chair and do whatever it took to save her. Fred did, and *Father* does.

Even in their flawed condition, dads can still bear a *Father* resemblance. The jolt that ran through Fred's heart when he first heard the bone-chilling scream from his daughter is not

dissimilar to what *Father* feels a thousand times a second when
you and I scream for help. *Father* not only hears the cries, He
feels the jolt. In fact, His ability to feel is the reason you and
I feel. Nerve endings are part of our design because we were
made in *Father's* image. Every physical body has millions of
nerve endings, each connected to two places—to our own
brain and to the heart of *Father*.

Father-Longing

Beneath this pattern of fatherlessness and father-wounds lies
something significant. The reason father-wounds are so raw
is because *Father*-longing is so real. Though *Father*-longing
is largely unconscious for most people, it is nonetheless
authentic, and when that spot inside you is violated or
cheapened, the pain is excruciating. Somewhere down deep
inside you is a longing only *Father* can satisfy, but when
your dad disappoints, it is easy to shut down and deny your
longing. The hole in your heart that longs for Him is for
real and your pain proves it. More than wanting a pay raise,
a promotion, or a stronger orgasm, the deepest desire you
have is for *Father*. The reason father-wounds run so deep is
because this tender spot inside your soul is sacred.

You will never be re-parented until you face your anger
against your father, or against *Father*. It is difficult to re-
parent a passive-aggressive child. I can assure you—what
you feel, *Father* feels; when you hurt, *Father* hurts; when
you need help, full-of-compassion *Father* is ready to run to
your side.

In order to comprehend the depth of the *Father's* hurt,
we need to understand that there is a rival father in the universe. The Bible calls him, "the father of lies" (John 8:44).

This liar primarily lies about *Father*. He is obsessed with bashing *Father*, and for good reason. Just think about it— Satan was the first orphan.

While an angel, or spirit-being, and not a human, he was nevertheless created by *Father*, and was even leading worship in *Father's* house. Yet his pride, selfish ambition, and rebellion got him permanently kicked out of the house, and he now roams the earth like a homeless drifter—a liar and father of lies, an orphan and father of orphans.

This imposter father gives exactly the opposite of what *Father* gives. Instead of acceptance, he gives rejection; rather than blessing, he gives curses; rather than healing, he causes hurt and pain; rather than trust, he devalues us by perpetuating distrust. This liar tells you that your father-wounds prove *Father* is untrustworthy.

Don't believe him! This liar wants to convince you that *Father* doesn't feel, doesn't hurt, and doesn't have compassion, but don't believe that either. Bottom line, he wants you to distrust *Father*.

Father's hurt will make more sense in the next chapter as we consider *Father's* Son. But first, I encourage you to pray a significant and far-reaching prayer. Knowing that *Father* hurts and that He feels what you feel, may make it easier to pray:

Father, re-parent me in Jesus' name.

4

Father's Son

YOUR QUEST for *Father* will invariably lead you to Jesus because Jesus is God with skin on. There is no way around it, if you want to find *Father*, you will find Him in the Son.

The entire ministry of Jesus on earth can be summed up in one word—*Father*. No one in history was more *Father*-focused than Jesus—and for good reason. He has been with *Father* for a gazillion years. Before there was time—before land or sea or goldfish—there was *Father*, Son, and Spirit. While *Father* is invisible, Jesus came as God with flesh and blood. He came from *Father*, on behalf of *Father*, to communicate *Father*, and to restore orphan hearts back to *Father*. From before the beginning, Jesus has been *Father's* only child, who alone could accurately call God *Father*. He came on a single mission: to expand *Father's* family, so orphans like me and you could legitimately know Him as *Father*, too.

When the Son came into the world, He talked *Father*, using the name in direct conversation or indirect reference no fewer than 170 times. He spoke of "Him who sent me" a whopping twenty-eight times. He saw the world into which He came as a sort of spiritual orphanage full of people with abandonment issues and father-wounds. It's not surprising that the orphans didn't know what to do with Him and greeted Him with hostility and resentment; but that didn't deter Him. Jesus knew there was a soft spot inside each orphan that only He could touch, a wound only He could heal, a gaping hole inside everyone's chest that craves recognition, acceptance, validation, and fathering that only He could fill.

God-Son

To understand the Son, you need to realize that He did not start when Jesus was born. As peculiar as it may sound, the Son was with *Father* for a long, long time; more accurately, He was with *Father* before there was time. God is eternal and existed when nothing else existed. Nothing else was needed. The Triune God was fully unified and thoroughly content within Himself. There was not a tinge of loneliness, boredom, void, or absence within God. Time had not yet been created, so there was no sense of hurry, delay, frustration, or tardiness. *Father*, Son, and Spirit live in the eternal present and love every minute of it.

It is no wonder Jesus said things like, "I am in the *Father* and the *Father* is in me" (John 14:10) and, "Whoever has seen me has seen the *Father*" (14:9) and, "I and thr *Father* are one" (10:30). As we have already agreed, we don't need *Father for Dummies*, and we don't want *Son for Dummies* either. Though it will challenge your IQ to keep pace with *Father*'s wisdom, the dynamic interface between *Father* and Son is more than intriguing—it's captivating.

Every title given to Jesus in *Father*'s book—and there are many—are insightful to help unlock the genius of God. In order to zero in on a healthy understanding of Jesus, we will consider only two strategic names or titles appropriately assigned to Him—Son and Word. Both titles not only accurately identify His distinct identity, they help pinpoint nuances of His mission.

The primary name or title used in reference to Jesus is Son, used over two-hundred times in the Gospels. Perhaps the most familiar verse in the entire Bible is John 3:16: "For God so loved the world, that he gave his only [*monogenes*] Son, that whoever believes in him should not perish but have eternal life." While this verse is familiar, the translation is incomplete. *Monogenus* is a significant word, but the unfortunate translation only misses the point.

JESUS IS THE ETERNALLY GENERATED ONE, CONTINUALLY COMING FROM THE FATHER.

The Greek word *mono* means only, but *mono* is not the word used here. This compound word *monogenus* carries a more significant punch: as we have said, *mono* means only, and *genus* means generated—the root word for genes, genome, generate, genesis. When you put this compound word together, you strike oil. *Monogenus* means that Jesus is the only one with God's genes; He is the eternally generated one, continually coming from the essence of the *Father*. In reality, *monogenus* has nothing to do with Jesus' birth in Bethlehem; it has everything to do with Him being continually generated from within *Father*. Jesus is the only Son with God's DNA. This is profound—Jesus is in the eternal state of perpetual generation from *Father*.

It is significant that one thousand years prior to Jesus' birth, *Father* used the same words to refer to His Son. "You are my Son; today I have begotten you" (Ps. 2:7). Because

God lives in the eternal present, as mind-stretching as it is, the Son has been continually generated from the *Father* long before His birth—from eternity. In a sense, *Father* says these words to the Son every day: "You are my Son; today I have begotten you." This means there is never a day when *Father* fails to generate the Son. This was true every day before there was time, and it will be true every day forward. When Jesus was physically born, it was simply an outward expression of an eternal reality.

Jesus is also identified as the Word: "In the beginning was the Word, and the Word was with God, and the Word was God" (John 1:1). This Word indicates an integral role the Son plays in the Godhead—of the three persons, it is the Son's role to communicate. When *Father* opens his mouth, so to speak, the Son comes out.

"In the beginning" is a phrase that bears a striking resemblance to the first words in *Father's* book: "In the beginning God created the heavens and the earth" (Gen. 1:1). It is no wonder that the next words in John's Gospel further link itself to the creation account in Genesis: "He was in the beginning with God. All things were made through him, and without him was not any thing made that was made" (John 1:2–3). To avoid ambiguity regarding the identity of the Word, John connects the dots even more explicitly when he refers to Jesus' birth by saying, "And the Word became flesh and dwelt among us, and we have seen his glory, glory as of the only Son from the *Father*, full of grace and truth" (1:14).

This Word is none other than the Son who is assigned the distinct role of clearly communicating *Father*. John adds, "No one has ever seen God; the only God, who is at the *Father's* side, he has made him known [*exegeomai*]" (1:18).

Exegeomai is another compound word that means to take what is hidden deep inside and bring it into plain sight. This indicates that it is the Son's unique role to take what is hidden, deep inside *Father*, and draw it out so you and I can see Him in plain view. The one who is *mono-genus*, continually sent from within *Father*, is also *exe-geomai*, continually taking from within *Father* and making it known. Both roles obviously put Jesus in a league all His own. No one else is able to come from the guts and essence of *Father* and draw Him out. *Father* emphasizes the distinct superiority of His Son as His primary communicator when He says:

> Long ago, at many times and in many ways, God spoke to our fathers by the prophets, but in these last days he has spoken to us by his Son, whom he appointed the heir of all things, through whom also he created the world. He is the radiance of the glory of God and the exact imprint of his nature, and he upholds the universe by the word of his power. (Heb. 1:1–3)

The best the prophets could do was speak about *Father*; but the Son comes from within *Father* and gives a better word.

These two distinct titles—Son and Word—highlight two exclusive roles that only Jesus fulfills: He is the only generated Son, who is continually flowing from *Father*; and He is the Word, who clearly communicates *Father*. Keep in mind that Jesus "is the same yesterday and today and forever" (13:8) which means everything we see in Him now will always be true of Him.

Man-Son

Everything we read about Jesus' life in the four Gospels is a direct expression of *Father*. Everything he did, *Father* did:

"The Son can do nothing of his own accord, but only what he sees the *Father* doing. For whatever the *Father* does, that the Son does likewise" (John 5:19); everything He said, *Father* said: "I do nothing on my own authority, but speak just as the *Father* has taught me" (8:28); every relationship He developed, *Father* gave Him: "No one can come to me unless the *Father* who sent me draws him" (6:44).

Jesus explained the secret behind His supernatural earth-walk by quoting *Father's* words:

> The Spirit of the Lord is upon me,
>> because he has anointed me
>> to proclaim good news to the poor.
> He has sent me to proclaim liberty to the captives
>> and recovering of sight to the blind,
>> to set at liberty those who are oppressed,
> to proclaim the year of the Lord's favor.
>
> (Luke 4:18–19)

Notice how Jesus attributed His potency to the Spirit. While we have already established the dynamic interface between *Father* and Son, we now discover more than a dynamic duo; we find in God a powerful trifecta. The Spirit of God sent by *Father* empowers the Son. This means that the miracles Jesus performed were not performed out of His own deity, but out of His Spirit-anointed humanity.

The compassion we have seen in *Father* is now oozing from every pore of the Son. Jesus took compassion and made it an art form. The Gospels show Him as a man who was frequently "moved with compassion [*splachnon*]."[1] *Splachnon* is a funny word that is difficult to pronounce. (It requires a hard guttural noise that sounds like you are trying clear the phlegm from the back of your throat, and it is hard to say without spitting on the person in front of you.) *Splachnon* refers to the tummy—the guts, intestines, liver, and bowels of a person. When Jesus was moved with compassion, it literally means His lower abdomen was churning in a circular motion. The cool thing about *splachnon* is you can't fake it. It's not superficial or external. It starts deep in your gut so that you either have it, or you don't. Jesus had compassion more than anyone because He was *Father* with skin on. Whenever Jesus was moved with compassion, miracles happened: He fed 5,000 hungry people, healed leprous skin and blind eyes, and gave value to a misfit who had been filled with self-hatred, all in response to His compassion.

One of Jesus' compassion moments was captured this way: "When he saw the crowds, he had compassion [*splachnon*] for them, because they were harassed and helpless, like sheep without a shepherd" (Matt. 9:36.) Many people are intimidated by crowds, but not Jesus. When He saw masses of people, His *splachnon* started doing backflips like Simone Biles. He looked beneath the surface and saw people desperate and destitute. He saw people looking as if they had been filleted alive, skinless and exposed, hurting and helpless, lost and hopeless, like sheep without a shepherd, like hearts without a home. This same *splachnon* is what He demonstrates today when He looks at me and you.

When Jesus was born, something highly significant took place—something bigger than a gender reveal or a birth announcement. The Son, who was already fully God, now for the first time becomes fully human. The eternal God who previously existed invisibly for all eternity, now, for the first time, gets a physical body. The significance of the body is profound. His body not only made Him visible, it links

Him inseparably, for better and for worse, to our humanity. What we feel, He feels; our bruises are His bruises; our needs become His needs.

Wounded Son

Jesus' physical body served an additional purpose. More than simply being able to feel, Jesus' body was able to bleed. Jesus needed a body, because no body, no blood; no blood, no sacrifice; no sacrifice, no forgiveness; no forgiveness, no adoption; no adoption, no family; no family, no access to *Father*. In the brilliance of *Father's* strategy, in order to expand the family and include you and me, He knew His Son would not only need to be born with human skin, He needed to die. The only One who could rightfully call Him *Father* would need to die so that orphans like us could be adopted as daughters and sons.

> **FOR JESUS TO BE EXECUTED BY CRUCIFIXION WAS NOTHING SHORT OF SCANDALOUS.**

The moment of Jesus' death was indescribably barbaric. Crucifixion is listed as the number one most torturous and gruesome form of execution ever developed. The Romans loved the public humiliation of lynching, but they thought death by hanging or the executioner's axe was much too quick and painless, so they invented this inhumane process because, while they enjoyed the public humiliation of death by hanging, they wanted to increase the pain and extend the agony.

Crucifixion represents the worst in human nature: It gave a front row seat to any twisted soul who got their jollies out of watching the unthinkable agony. For Jesus to be executed in this inhumane way was nothing short of scandalous. It was scandalous that people would treat him like an animal; it was scandalous that no one tried to stop it—not the Jewish religious leaders, not the Roman political leaders, and not even his disciples; it was scandalous that Jesus submitted to it; and it was scandalous that the *Father* watched it happen. The crucifixion of Jesus was the most violent, unjust moment in human history.

This scandalous event culminated when Christ screamed the infamous words, "*Eli, Eli, lema sabachthani?*" These words were spoken in Aramaic, Jesus' heart language, and they meant, "My God, my God, why have you forsaken me?" (Matt. 27:46). These were orphan words of abandonment, rejection, painful separation, and alienation.

This is literally the first time in eternity that Jesus spoke to God without addressing Him as *Father*. In fact, two other times while on the cross, He used the name *Father* in prayer: "*Father*, forgive them, for they know not what they do" (Luke 23:34) and "*Father*, into your hands I commit my spirit" (23:46), but not this time. For the first time, He felt forsaken, abandoned; he literally felt a father-wound. No wonder the sky literally turned pitch black from noon to 3 p.m.[2]

If you look closely at Christ on the cross, you notice something else: *You* are there, too. If a coroner or crime scene investigator had been able to do an autopsy on Jesus' mangled body, my DNA would be found in his wounds, and so would yours.

There is an ongoing debate over who is responsible for Jesus' execution. Was it: A) the Romans? B) the Jews? or C) the crowds? Every few years, scholars resurface the debate and publish their opinions in *Time, Newsweek*, or some university journal. The answer, however, is: D) All of the above.

Father says, "He was pierced for our transgressions; he was crushed for our iniquities" (Isa. 53:5). This means that the mangled body of Jesus is full of your own DNA. The cross becomes the point of contact between heaven and earth. The cross represents the worst of humanity and the best of *Father*—the place where our rebellious, twisted pride murders the Son, and where *Father* takes it.

The apostle Paul called the cross a scandal: "We preach Christ crucified, a stumbling block [*scandalon*]" (1 Cor. 1:23). The cross was a scandal no matter how you look at it: It was a scandal for those who killed Jesus, thinking they were putting an end to Him; it was a scandal for Jesus who was utterly innocent; it was a scandal for *Father* who watched His Son mangled; and it was a scandal for us because our fingerprints were found at the crime scene. The word *scandalon* refers to a movable stick that served as the trigger in a trap used to catch prey. Those who killed Jesus were caught in the trap of *Father*'s eternal plan; Jesus was caught in the trap of fulfilling *Father*'s plan; you and I were caught in the trap because we were exposed as desperately needing the cross; and *Father* is smiling as He is caught in the middle of His perfectly premeditated trap. Seeing your sin in Jesus is where you step on *Father*'s trap-stick and become wonderfully caught. The cross is *Father*'s trap-stick intentionally placed in your path to catch you because the only way you can face your sin is to see the Son. If you look into your own soul, it's too dark—more horrifying and traumatizing than any Stephen King novel. Plus, when you look inside your soul, you can't see straight—sin is self-deceiving—what crawls around inside your heart is self-deceiving. You look to the Son, however, and you not only see yourself clearly, you can now handle the sight because it is surrounded by the loving wounds of Jesus. If you look within yourself, you will see your sin and feel hopeless; if you look at the Son, you will see your sins and feel hope-filled. As grotesque as it is, the cross is redemptive.

When you look at the scandalous wisdom of *Father*, you quickly see that what got Jesus killed was actually the reason for which He came. Read carefully the motivation of His murderers: "This was why the Jews were seeking all the more to kill him, because not only was he breaking the Sabbath, but he was even calling God his own *Father*, making himself equal with God" (John 5:18). This means that what actually got Jesus killed—calling God *Father*—was the reason *Father* sent His Son in the first place.

You might think Jesus' death was a last-ditch effort. You may think, since humanity made such a mess of things, *Father* had no other option but to sacrifice His Son on the cross, almost settling for second best. Not a chance. The cross was an essential plank in *Father's* masterplan from the beginning—long before there were oceans, mountains, and horned toads. The phrase "the foundation of the world" is used ten times in the New Testament, and it refers to events prior to and during the beginning of time. As mind-boggling as it sounds, Jesus was chosen to shed His blood as sacrificial payment for our sins "before the foundation of the world"(1 Pet. 1:20), and somehow, not only was He chosen before the world was formed, it goes as far as saying, "The Lamb [was] slain from the foundation of the world" (Rev. 13:8, KJV). And as if that is not mind-boggling enough, you and I were also chosen to be in *Father's* family "before the foundation of the world" (Eph. 1:4).

Validation

The ugliness of the cross tells only half the redemption story—the human half. The rest of the story is *Father's* half. While people brutally murdered the Son, *Father* gloriously raised Him and gave Him the seat of honor. The validation of the Son is a double validation: He brought Jesus' dead body back to life, and then a month later elevated His body all the way up to heaven. The resurrection-validation of Christ was the proof that His payment for our adoption was complete; the ascension-validation was the proof that *Father's* strategic plan was an overwhelming success. *Father* explains it this way:

> This Jesus God raised up, and of that we all are witnesses. Being therefore exalted at the right hand of God, and having received from the *Father* the promise of the Holy Spirit, he has poured out this that you yourselves are seeing and hearing. (Acts 2:32–33)

Notice the fluidity and triunity of God: *Father* raised the Son; He exalted Him to sit down at His right hand; *Father* gives the Son the Spirit; and the Son gives the Spirit to God's people. Cool.

The ascension of Christ is the most overlooked essential Christian doctrine. Christian tradition has done well to celebrate the birth of Jesus at Christmas. It celebrates the crucifixion of Jesus by consistently sharing the Lord's Supper. It celebrates the resurrection of Jesus at Easter. But it does a lousy job celebrating the Ascension. Think about it: the Son was a baby for a few months; He was crucified for a few hours; He was raised to walk the earth for only forty days; but He has been ascended and glorified for two thousand years!

This ascended, glorified, validated, anointed, and anointing Christ is the total package. The ascended Christ affirms the Incarnation, because He still has the body from His birth; He affirms the Crucifixion because He still bears the nailprints in His hands and feet; He affirms the Resurrection because He is very much alive.

> **TODAY, JESUS IS SEATED AT THE RIGHT HAND OF FATHER, THE MEDIATOR BETWEEN US AND GOD.**

Today, Jesus is not a baby lying in a manger; He is not a mangled man hanging from a cross; He is not simply walking the earth as the Resurrected One. He is seated at the right hand of *Father*, where He lives to pray for us as the Mediator between us and God. The ascended, glorified, validated Christ is the accurate picture of Jesus today.

Let's summarize what we have learned so far about the Son's relationship with *Father*.

- Jesus knew His identity was in *Father*.[3]
- He knew He was loved and blessed by *Father*;[4] and He was secure, knowing that *Father* would provide for all His needs and answer all His prayers.[5]
- He knew His calling—that *Father* sent Him on mission.[6]
- He received the Holy Spirit from *Father*.[7]
- Jesus loved *Father*, and always obeyed *Father*.[8]

One Way

The scandal of Christ qualifies Him as the one and only Redeemer, Savior, Messiah. This one-and-only aspect of Christ is still a snag for many would-be followers. Mel

Gibson's film *The Passion of the Christ* provided a masterful portrait of the scourging and crucifixion of Jesus, and vividly demonstrates both the beauty and gruesomeness, the winsomeness and repulsiveness, the honor and shame of the cross. Toward the climax of the film, Jesus' words are appropriately scrolled across the screen: "I am the way, the truth, and the life. No one comes to the *Father* but by me" (John 14:6).

As much as you may be inspired by Jesus' sacrifice, the words, "No one comes to the *Father* but by me" may strike you as exclusionary. In our pluralistic society, these words may sound restrictive. You may think, Isn't it kind of presumptuous of Jesus, to set Himself up as the solitary mediator between us and *Father*? After all the kindness and compassion we have seen in Jesus, perhaps this reads a bit like the fine-print on the bottom of the contract; almost like bait-and-switch.

These words only sound presumptuous or arrogant if we miss the essence of *Father* and Son. Sometimes we forget that Jesus is not running for the office of Savior against a few other candidates. There is no "Messiah draft day," like the NFL, with a bunch of athletes trying out for one position on the team. This is not a beauty contest, with Jesus standing among other contestants. This is not the Olympics, where Jesus is competing as Redeemer, standing on the middle, elevated platform with the gold metal around his neck, between the runners-up who get silver and bronze. The Son stands alone—no rivals, no opponents, no contestants, no runners-up, no honorable mentions.

Father and Son do, in fact, have a categorically exclusive relationship. As we have seen, Jesus is in a league all by

Himself. When we read Jesus' words, "No one comes to the *Father* but by me," what should shock us is that we can be included at all. What should humble us and bring us to our knees is that you and I are even offered such access to *Father* in the first place. This makes perfect sense when you realize no one but Jesus has *Father* access to offer.

In a prophesy given seven hundred years prior to Jesus's birth, Isaiah predicted the coming of God's Son.

> For to us a child is born,
> to us a son is given;
> and the government shall be upon his shoulder,
> and his name shall be called
> Wonderful Counselor, Mighty God,
> Everlasting *Father*, Prince of Peace.
> Of the increase of his government and of peace
> there will be no end,
> on the throne of David and over his kingdom,
> to establish it and to uphold it
> with justice and with righteousness
> from this time forth and forevermore.
> The zeal of the Lord of hosts will do this.

Isa. 9:6–7

After all we have heard about the Son, Everlasting *Father* may sound surprising or even confusing. If Jesus is the Son, how can He also be the *Father*? you may wonder. The answer is profound: to the *Father*, He will always be the Son, but to us who are adopted into the family, Jesus is our *Dad*. Just as I will always be a son to my dad, yet a dad to my kids, so it is with Jesus. This reference to the Son also being the Everlasting *Father*, certainly reinforces the fact that Jesus is not only the Son of God, but God the Son.

It's now time to pray our six-word prayer. We could have potentially cut the prayer in half and reduced it to only three words: "*Father*, re-parent me," but such an abbreviation would make it useless. As we have learned, you don't have a chance in hell (and I use the word soberly) to encounter *Father* without Jesus. Nada. "In Jesus' name" may sound like a trite three-word religious jingle, but it's not. *Father* and Son are essentially and dynamically linked—they are a package deal. You get two for one, or you get none. You decide. It's time to pray:

Father, re-parent me in Jesus' name.

5

Father's Orphans

YOU AND I LIVE in an orphanage. If we were considering a name change for our planet, rather than Earth it could easily be called *Orphans R Us*.

An orphan is defined as a child under eighteen years of age who has lost one or both parents. According to UNICEF, there are 153 million orphans worldwide, and this number grows daily.[1] One out of fifty children in the United States are adopted, or close to 1.5 million children. Six in ten Americans have had personal experience with adoption which means that they themselves, or a close friend or family member was adopted, have an adopted child, or placed a child up for adoption. These numbers are gripping, but they only tell part of the orphan story.

Following the ugly dictatorship of Nicolae Ceausescu in Romania in 1989, tens of thousands of Romanian children were forced into poorly managed, state-run orphanages. Starving babies were locked in cages like animals. Their cries went unnoticed, and their diapers were rarely changed. Toddlers were strapped in highchairs for hours on end. These precious children, who had never known the love of a father and mother, nor even the hug of a caring adult, tragically became mentally and emotionally crippled. They developed what became known as reactive attachment disorder, a condition that influenced their personalities. They saw all adults as uncaring, abusive, and unreliable. These children were emotionally scarred and unable to function normally. Their anger became self-destructive, and most would never escape the pain of rejection, hyperactivity, learning disorders and compulsive tendencies to steal, lie, lash out, and hurt.

Because of the incredible psychological trauma, most did not live to see their twelfth birthday. They literally died from lack of love.

While you most likely have not suffered the depth of abandonment felt by these Romanian children, you may have your own set of father-wounds. Rheba McEntire described the raw reality of her lonely life with an ironic song title, "The Greatest Man I Never Knew." Millions of orphan souls can relate to the lyrics that lament a dad who never said, "I love you" because he thought she knew.[2]

Even for those who managed to escape father-wounds, there is the sinking feeling inside our soul that somehow we are damaged goods. In the words of author and world-class sea captain Jack Frost, "We all were born with an orphan heart that rejects parental authority and seeks to independently do everything our own way. The only humans that were not born with an orphan heart were Adam and Eve."[3] Frost goes on to write,

> When you possess the orphan heart, you never truly feel at home anywhere. You are afraid to trust, afraid of rejection, and afraid to open your heart to receive love. And unless you are able to receive love, you cannot unconditionally express love, even to your own family.[4]

Misery

Father-thinker George McDonald describes this common heart-cry as the one central misery of humanity: "The hardest, gladdest thing in the world is to cry *Father!* from a full heart. . . . The refusal to look up to God as our father is the one central longing in the whole human affair; the inability, the one central misery."[5] At the heart of life's misery is the refusal to embrace *Father*. This misery is in us and this misery is in *Father*. The misery of Jesus was to resolve the misery of both.

Victor Hugo did well to capture the misery of orphan scars when he published *Les Miserables*, a passionate story of social injustice, raw misery, broken dreams, love and sacrifice, forgiveness and redemption. It is not surprising that it was an instant success, not simply as a literary masterpiece, but as a social commentary. Hugo put his finger on a raw nerve: the universality of abandonment, and our need for *Father*. When it was produced as a musical, *Les Miserables* struck a chord world-wide.

Anne Hathaway played Fantine, a destitute factory worker forced to sell her hair and eventually her body to get enough money to purchase medication for her baby girl. Her side profession of prostitution, which was necessary to make ends meet, disgusted her, and when she refused to give a vile customer what he wanted, he brutalized her to the point of death.

The theme of misery was so deeply woven into the film that Hathaway admitted it took her months to physically recover. She said, "This isn't an invention, this is me honoring that this pain lives in this world."[6] One of the haunting, penetrating, gut-wrenching moments was when Hathaway sang the song, "I Dreamed a Dream." Her exhausted soul sang the stinging and unforgetting words of childhood dreams being raped and killed by the hell-like realities of life.[7] Even when Hathaway won an Oscar as supporting actress, she conceded,

> I felt very uncomfortable. I kind of lost my mind doing that movie and it hadn't come back yet. Then I had to stand up in front of people and feel something I didn't feel which is uncomplicated happiness. . . . I felt wrong that I was standing there in a gown that cost more than some people are going to see in their lifetime and winning an award to portray pain that still felt very much a part of our collective experience as human beings.[8]

> ## *LES MISERABLES* IS A STORY OF HUMAN MISERY, BUT ALSO OF REDEMPTION —A STORY OF *FATHER*.

Misery was deeply embedded in the story, but redemption was even more dominant. The life story of the main character, Jean Valjean, was one of genuine loss followed by authentic redemption. Branded as a thief, he was given a second chance by changing his identity. He went on to forgive his taskmaster prison guard and rescue Fantine's daughter from an abusive home, giving her hope of a better life. *Les Miserables* is a story of human misery and abandonment, yet it is also a story of redemption—a story of *Father*. It is no wonder the film was seen by over 60 million people in forty-two countries. The authentic story of misery and redemption will always have an audience.

Orphans R Us

World history is full of notable orphans, including Steve Jobs, John Lennon, Marilyn Monroe, Babe Ruth, Ingrid Bergman, Ice-T, George Lopez, Eleanor Roosevelt, Leo Tolstoy, Jack

Nicolson, Nichole Richie, Faith Hill, Bill Clinton, Collin Kaepernick, Gerald Ford, Nancy Reagan, Nelson Mandela, and even Saint Nicolas (aka Santa Claus).

Fictional orphans include Harry Potter, Batman and Robin, James Bond, Anne Shirley (*Anne of Green Gables*), Tarzan, Clark Kent (Superman), Avatar, Kyoshi, the Lone Ranger, Huckleberry Finn, the Mandalorian, Spiderman, Supergirl, and Oliver Twist.

Disney's animated movies are also full of orphans. More than half (56 out of 104) of all the Disney animated films since 1957 have a dead or missing parent.

- Pinocchio, Tarzan, Snow White, Cinderella, Rapunzel, Mowgli in *The Jungle Book*, Aladdin, Simba in *The Lion King*, Linguini in *Ratatouille*, and Paddington Bear are all orphans.

- Peter Pan is a "lost boy," essentially an orphan.

- In *Beauty and the Beast*, Belle's mom is missing, and her dad is virtually useless.

- Bambi's mom is unforgettably killed, and his dad is missing.

- In *Finding Nemo*, Nemo's mom is killed by a barracuda and his dad, while well meaning, is ineffective.

- In *Frozen*, both parents of Elsa and Anna are lost at sea.

- In *101 Dalmatians*, Perdita cares for 84 orphan puppies.

These animated films have been some of the most watched films in the history of cinematography, for one reason— they strike a chord in every orphan heart on earth. Orphan runs through humanity like blood through our veins. Disney movies are also preoccupied with this orphan thing because the human heart longs for *Father*. Some movie critics have made a big deal over the conspicuous absence of strong dads in Disney movies, trying to hatch some kind of conspiracy theory. But it's not conspiracy, it's human nature—Orphans R Us.

Notable Orphans

Marilyn Monroe was born Norma Jeane Mortenson and grew up without a mother or father. She told stories about being raped and sexually abused as a child of only eleven years. To escape the abuse, she married at age sixteen. As an adult she suffered from severe depression which today would be called bipolar disease. She once said in desperation, "I am trying to find myself. Sometimes that's not easy."[9]

As the top-billed actress of the day, with her films grossing $200 million (equivalent to $2 billion today), her screen image defied reality. In her lifetime, and to this day, her photos remain some of the most iconic in history. Few people realize that behind her smile was a lost little girl. She had been shuffled from one foster home to another.

At the peak of her career, a reporter from the *New York Times* interviewed her and asked, "Did you ever feel loved by any of the foster families with whom you lived?" "Once," she replied, "When I was about seven or eight. The woman I was living with was putting on makeup, and I was watching her. She was in a happy mood, so she reached over and patted my cheeks with the rouge…" Then she added with tears in her eyes, "For that moment, I felt loved by her."[10]

Marilyn Monroe was one of the most photographed women on earth, yet people were so transfixed with her skin, they never saw the pain she felt beneath her skin. It is tragic to think of how many orphans feel such loneliness, emptiness, void—the absence of love. Even a pretty face cannot hide the lonely tears of a wounded heart.

John Lennon was one of the greatest songwriters in history. Born in Liverpool, England and raised by his aunt and uncle, he was a self-taught guitarist. John and his friend Paul McCartney became the most successful songwriters of all time. John was an orphan.

Steve Jobs, one of the most brilliant inventors of our age, was also an orphan. Jobs said, "The ones who are crazy enough to think they can change the world, are the ones who do."[11] He not only built Apple Computer with his buddy Steve Wozniak but developed it into a dynasty which in June 2019 was worth $750 billion, more than Google and Microsoft combined. In the definitive biography, *Steve Jobs*, Walter Isaacson showed both the genius and the flaws of a person who insisted on perfection. Steve was an orphan.

Babe Ruth was arguably the greatest baseball player in history. He was born George Herman Ruth in Baltimore, Maryland. As a youth, he was a troublemaker, a hard drinker who threw tomatoes at police. His parents couldn't control him, so at age seven they sent him to be raised by the no-nonsense-nuns at Saint Mary's Industrial School for Boys, part orphanage and part trade school.

George spent the next eleven years there, and became the star pitcher on the school's baseball team. He was soon signed by Jack Dempsey, owner of the city's minor league team, the Baltimore Orioles. Dempsey became Ruth's legal guardian until he turned twenty-one. During this time, the owner and player became very close, almost father and son, and players referred to Ruth as "Jack's Babe," and the nickname stuck. Soon the world would be introduced to a man who would become the greatest baseball player of all time. Babe Ruth was an orphan.

Jamie Foxx was born Eric Bishop and was put up for adoption soon after birth. His finely developed sense of humor led him to a career in comedy, and he took the name of his favorite comedian, Redd Foxx. Jamie was an orphan.

> ## WHILE WE MAY NOT FIT THE DEFINITION OF AN ORPHAN, WE ARE ALL ORPHAN-HEARTED.

Sylvester Stallone was technically not an orphan, but he was raised in an extraordinarily strict home. By the time he was twelve years old, he had been kicked out of thirteen schools and broken eleven bones. As a child he had rickets (a vitamin deficiency that affects bone development) and was badly bullied. He recalls his dad being physically abusive and his mom rarely showing him affection. When he was fifteen, Stallone was told that his brain was dormant. Despite his limitations, Sylvester Stallone has become one of the most elite A-list actors and film writers in Hollywood history.

Less Notable

These true stories of notable orphans only begin to tell our story. While we may not fit the definition of an orphan as defined by UNICEF, we are all orphan-hearted. The orphan heart is lonely, abandoned, independent, contentious, competitive, defensive, territorial, surviving, hostile, jealous, envious, without any sense of belonging, poor, and homeless. We can all appreciate a healthy spirit of competition, but for orphans, competition is ugly—full of jealousy, envy, and an "I'm-better-than-you, I-will-crush-you-like-a-grape" attitude. Unhealthy competition is rooted in the orphan spirit.

The chronic flaw of our humanity is that, like orphans, we are always keeping score. We are our strictest referee. Thomas Merton, one of the most effective spiritual guides in our generation, advises, "Quit keeping score all together and surrender ourselves with all our sinfulness to God who sees neither the score nor the scorekeeper but only his child redeemed by Christ."[12] A newspaper once asked its readers a straightforward question: "What's wrong with the world?" The great Christian thinker G.K. Chesterton wrote a brief letter of response: "Dear Sirs, I am. Sincerely Yours, G.K. Chesterton."[13] We would all do well to have such a healthy dose of humility.

The orphan spirit crawls around the earth breathing its ideology into every sector of society. Orphan thinking is rampant from Wall Street to Silicon Valley to Hollywood—greed, craving, lust, pride, and competition suck life from us all. It may be helpful to clarify the qualities normally found in orphans. You may even see reflections of these qualities, to a greater or lesser extent, in your own life.

- Rejection
- Distrust
- Abandonment
- Alienation
- Loneliness
- Anxiety/fear
- Hopelessness

- Anger/rage
- Poverty
- Hypersensitivity
- Hurts/wounds/pain
- Homelessness
- Abuse
- Worthlessness

- Territorialism
- Curses
- Self-hatred
- Insignificance
- Insecurity
- Wandering
- Fear of Death

Psychologists call these qualities an orphan mentality. If you are unfamiliar with the term, do an internet search—you will be amazed how many articles have been written on the topic. Fighting the orphan mentality or the orphan spirit is a losing battle until you have something greater—a higher power—with which to fight. The orphan mentality is far more transcendent than simply lacking a relationship with your biological parents; it's about finding *Father*.

Dennis Rodman was a culture icon of the NBA champion Chicago Bulls. He was also an enigma—he had incredible skill and intelligence, but he would show up late for practice, underperform, and rarely seemed to take himself seriously. When he stepped on the court, however, he became a rebounding machine and a defensive maniac—he always found his way into the heads of the opposing players. In 911 NBA games, he scored 6,683 points and grabbed 11,954 rebounds, which translates into 13.1 rebounds per game in only 31.7 minutes of playing time per game. NBA.com heralds Rodman as, "Arguably the best rebounding forward in NBA history."[14] To a coach like Phil Jackson, who found the secret of harnessing Rodman's potential, Dennis was worth his weight in gold.

Behind his signature multicolored hairstyles, recklessness, late-night escapades, substance abuse, and frequent violent outbursts, was a deeper issue. It may have had something to do with the fact that Dennis was one of twenty-nine children, fathered by a man with sixteen different women.[15] Behind the tats, hair colors, and body piercing lives a man without a dad, or at least one whom he had not seen for forty-two years. For a brief moment in July 2012, Philander Rodman, Jr., Dennis' dad, got to see his son play basketball at an exhibition game. Sadly, the meeting lasted only a few minutes. They said hi, exchanged pleasantries, shook hands, and said goodbye, all in a matter of moments.[16]

Underneath Rodman's persona, he has a heart, and he has three children of his own—Alexis, Dennis Jr., and Trinity.[17] Many have wondered, *What is it like to have Dennis Rodman as your dad?* After thirty days in a rehab facility following a DUI, Rodman admitted, "I want to see my kids grow up. I just needed to stop partying, take a step back and get my life in order."[18]

He knows his kids are his blessings. He even congratulated his daughter Trinity on Instagram and said, "I love you very much."[19] It's a start. His relationship with his children seems to be moving in the right direction. Dennis Rodman is a work in progress. Aren't we all?

From the moment of birth, when we cry "Whaaaaaah!" we are crying for *Father*. One of my favorite *Father* names in the Bible is "*Father* of the fatherless" (Ps. 68:5). This endearing title certainly includes those who have had the misfortune of losing dad or mom, but it also includes those of us with orphan hearts. *Father* is for all of us. He is the *Dad* of all the downtrodden, marginalized, less-than-notable, and overlooked orphans like you and me.

As incredible as it sounds, God Almighty wants to parent you, and He wants to start today. No tryouts, no auditions, no application process—just come as you are. Tats, multicolored hair—nothing can disqualify you from *Father's* love.

When you are ready, He is waiting for you to genuinely ask:

Father, re-parent me in Jesus' name.

6

Father's Adoption

THERE IS NO greater misery than being orphan-hearted, and there is no greater joy than adoption. Every orphan is looking for home, and every orphan-heart is longing for *Father*.

When *Father* sent His Son to our human orphanage, He did so to expand His family. It should come as no surprise that on the last night of His life, when He was preparing to pay for our adoption, Jesus said to His disciples, "I will not leave you as orphans" (John 14:18).

Fatherlessness is more of a global crisis than we realize. In the United States, of the 64 million men who have fathered children, only 26.5 million are currently part of a home where they are in any way active fathers in their children's lives. Over one-third of the children in the United States are growing up without a dad. According to the US Department of Justice, 70% of inmates are fatherless, and 85% of juveniles.[1]

Fatherless children are five times as likely to commit suicide, 209% more likely to use drugs, thirty-two times more likely to run away from home, twenty times more likely to have behavioral disorders, fourteen times more likely to rape someone, and nine times more likely to drop out of school.[2]

When Bob Dylan croons about being homeless, all alone and unknown in his unforgettable song "Like a Rolling Stone," he is singing for all of us.[3] But this is only the tip of the iceberg. Underneath the icecap of fatherlessness is the iceberg of *Father*lessness.

Adoption

The words "I will not leave you as orphans" summarize Jesus' mission. As we have said, He came into our human orphanage to expand *Father*'s family. Anyone who has been through the adoption process knows just how arduous adoption is. Beyond the heartache and heartbreak, there are mountains of paperwork, countless courtroom visits, legal interviews, inspections, plus all the emotional blood, sweat, and tears.

But for Jesus, it was unthinkably worse. In order for the only Son to be able to adopt you and me into *Father*'s family, He needed to taste rejection and abandonment. There may be 153 million fatherless children in the world, but there are billions of *Father*less children. As the Bible says, we "groan inwardly as we wait eagerly for adoption [*huiothesia*] as sons" (Rom. 8:23).

Huiothesia is a beautiful word for adoption. The root of the word is *huio* which means mature son, or to become a full-fledged son with all rights and privileges. Don't allow the gender-specific terminology to confuse you—the Bible is not written by male chauvinists. Adoption as sons is significant and not at all demeaning to women. In the first century, Middle Eastern women would not have received an equal inheritance. The very fact that the Bible explicitly states that every child—male and female—receives adoption as sons means they all receive an equal share of the inheritance. Adoption as sons, therefore, is not demeaning, but honoring and elevating for women.

Make It Legal

Adoption must be legal in order for it to stick. No one wants to go through the tedious, legal process only to default by some technicality. For this reason, *Father* was tedious and exacting when it came to securing your adoption. Let the record show: "When the fullness of time had come, God sent forth his Son, born of woman, born under the law, to redeem those who were under the law, so that we might receive adoption as sons [*huiothesia*]" (Gal. 4:4–5).

> IN ROMAN LAW, ADOPTION WAS
> A DEFINING MOMENT WITH
> FAR-REACHING CONSEQUENCES.

The legality of adoption was so important that at the moment it became official, the Roman magistrate would actually shout the word *huiothesia*! As he prepared to drop his gavel, he would lean back, smile from ear to ear, and loudly declare the joyful proclamation, "*Huiothesia*! You are now an adopted son!" This was a defining moment with far-reaching consequences.

It is important to understand that first-century orphans almost invariably became slaves. In order to avoid slavery, orphans frequently developed a false identity. Simon Tugwell gives significant insight in his book *The Beatitudes*:

> And so, like runaway slaves, we either flee our own reality or manufacture a false self which is mostly admirable, mildly

prepossessing, and superficially happy. We hide what we know or feel ourselves to be (which we assume to be unacceptable and unlovable) behind some kind of appearance which we hope will be more pleasing. We hide behind pretty faces which we put on for the benefit of our public. And in time we may even come to forget that we are hiding, and think that our assumed pretty face is what we really look like.[4]

In the Roman world, because so many orphans became slaves, when a slave was legally adopted, three things took place:

1. The adopted slave was set free, and all children of that slave were also freed;

2. The adopted child received a full inheritance, equal to the other children in the house;

3. All previous debts were immediately canceled.

When an orphan-slave was legally adopted in the Roman world, it was a moment of joyful celebration for the whole community. Similarly, there is a joyful celebration in heaven when a soul is legally adopted.

One of the greatest Christian thinkers in the past hundred years, J. I. Packer wrote extensively on adoption and the fatherhood of God. In his bestselling book, *Knowing God*, he beautifully described it this way:

Adoption is a family idea, conceived in terms of love, and viewing God as father. In adoption, God takes us into his family and fellowship, and establishes us as his children and heirs. Closeness, affection, and generosity are at the heart of the relationship. To be right with God the judge is a great thing, but to be loved and cared for by God is greater.[5]

Re-birth

Adoption is a fitting word picture that describes the legal transaction of a person who is welcomed into *Father's* family; re-birth is a fitting word picture that describes the inner change of heart.

Late one night, Jesus spoke with a theological genius known as Nicodemus: "Truly, truly, I say to you, unless one is born again he cannot see the kingdom of God" (John 3:3). Being re-born sounded so intriguing, the seasoned theologian asked, "How can a man be born when he is old? Can he enter a second time into his mother's womb and be born?" (3:4).

In response, Jesus clarified: "Truly, truly, I say to you, unless one is born of water and the Spirit, he cannot enter the kingdom of God. That which is born of the flesh is flesh, and that which is born of the Spirit is spirit" (3:5–7).

Notice the critical distinction: Physical life requires physical birth, and spirit-life requires spirit-birth—the re-birth of the human spirit, which is only possible by the God Spirit.

Jesus' emphasis on the human spirit is critical. For most people born in the western world, we deny the spirit. We put so much emphasis on the body and the soul that we lack any type of vocabulary to even describe the spirit, and for good reason: when we are physically born, our spirit is still-born. It's dead. This is precisely why Jesus said, "You must be born again."

You and I are trinitarian, just as God is: He is *Father*, Son, and Spirit, and we are spirit, soul, and body. We are well familiar with our physical body; we are reasonably familiar with the soul—the mind, will, and emotions; but when it comes to the spirit, we are ignoramuses. Because your spirit was dead on arrival, it requires re-birth. It is this portion of yourself that is eternal—where you know *Father*, where you talk with *Father*, and where *Father* talks to you.

Re-birth is the basis of your relationship with *Father* because re-birth starts on the inside—in your spirit. Since it is the spirit that is re-born, it is the spirit that is re-parented. Religious Nicodemus knew better than just about anyone how to follow *Father* externally, but he did not have a clue how to follow *Father* internally. This revelation of re-birth was an eye-opener for him, and it may be an eye-opener for you.

When it comes to your adoption and your re-birth, you want to be certain that the transaction has taken place. There is nothing more unsettling for an orphan than to feel insecure about the legality of the adoption papers. You do not want to worry about whether or not your spirit adoption is legal. He wants you to have the assurance of your re-birth. You want to know for certain that when you die you will go to heaven, and more importantly, you want to know for certain that you are now *Father's* child with all rights and privileges. This Spirit of adoption as sons gives you the ability in the pit of your spirit to cry, *Abba, Daddy*. *Father* said:

> And this is the testimony, that God gave us eternal life, and this life is in his Son. Whoever has the Son has life; whoever does not have the Son of God does not have life. I write these things to you who believe in the name of the Son of God, that you may know that you have eternal life. (1 John 5:11–13)

When I was a college student, I flew from Newark to Chicago to return to campus after winter break. It was the most turbulent flight of my life. Briefcases were flying around the cabin; flight attendants were landing on passenger's laps; people were screaming. At that moment I realized that if the plane went down, I was not sure I was going up.

When we finally landed and exited the plane, I resolved to make sure I had the assurance of salvation. When I got to my apartment, I grabbed my Bible and a large metal railroad stake and went outside to be all alone with God. I knelt down in the snow, opened my Bible, and read First John 5:11–13. I then prayed a very simple prayer. I told *Father* that I believed in the Son. I took Jesus as my Savior and I received the Spirit of adoption. As a visible declaration of my faith, I pounded the railroad stake deep into the ground.

I knew that the stake I drove into the ground to mark that moment was not what saved me; it was the stakes that were driven into Jesus that purchased my adoption. But my stake was a declaration of my claim on Jesus' blood sacrifice for me, and it helped me mark the date of my prayer, so that if the enemy of my soul would ever try to accuse me and tell me that I wasn't *Father's* child, or that I wasn't good enough, I could always point back to the stake I drove into the ground that day. At that moment, I received the assurance of my salvation, that I was now legally adopted with all rights and privileges. I further knew that the spirit within me was now re-born.

Father wants to give you a similar moment. Keep in mind that adoption is not something you earn or deserve. It's not a lottery system with a vast number of orphans elbowing for a limited number of spots. *Father* does not pick a lucky number out of a hat. There is no audition or try-outs. You don't need to struggle through a lengthy application process. There is no entrance exam you need to pass. You don't need to write an impressive essay to prove your worth or justify your existence. While everything rides on the success of your adoption, none of it rests on your shoulders. *Father* already has you covered. As we have said, He sent His Son to purchase your adoption. Your adoption papers are already filled out. Your essay has been written. Your processing fee has been paid in full. When you take the Son, your spirit is re-born and your adoption is complete.

> ## As important as it is to *be Abba's* child, it is also important to *know* you are *Abba's* child.

It's hard to get any traction in prayer until you are confident that you are, in fact, *Abba's* child. Many children lose sleep over feeling insecure and unwanted, and too many of *Abba's* children feel insecure over their salvation. As important as it is to *be Abba's* child, it is also important to *know* you are *Abba's* child. Right now, you can receive your rebirth and the assurance of your adoption. I encourage you to pray this prayer:

> *Father, I need to know for certain right now that I am reborn as Your adopted child—I need to know for certain that when I die, I will be with You forever. The Bible says, "I write these things to you who believe in the name of the Son of God, that you may know that you have eternal life." Right now, I declare that I believe that Jesus is the Son of God, and on the basis of this Bible verse, I receive the re-birth of my spirit and I receive my adoption into Your family, in Jesus' name. I mark this day as the day of my salvation. I not only receive*

salvation in the name of the Lord Jesus Christ, I receive the assurance of my salvation. Today I know for certain that I am Your child and I will be with You forever. Amen.

If you just prayed this prayer and received adoption and re-birth, let me be the first to say, congratulations! As *Father* says, "Now is the favorable time; behold, now is the day of salvation" (2 Cor. 6:2).

First-century slave-orphans wanted to make sure their adoption was legal so that they could hear the thrilling word *huiothesia*, "You are now an adopted son!" In the same way, you want to make sure your adoption is legal. You want to hear *Father* cry, "*Huiothesia!*" and you want to have the joy of being able to cry out from your belly, "*Abba! Father!*"

As the Roman magistrate robustly declared *huiothesia*, God gives you and me a word to joyfully declare—*Abba!* In the words of the apostle Paul, "And because you are sons, God has sent the Spirit of his Son into our hearts, crying, '*Abba! Father!*' So you are no longer a slave, but a son, and if a son, then an heir through God" (Gal. 4:6–7).

To help you appreciate the significance of what happens when you receive the Son, I encourage you to carefully read this story.

A wealthy man and his son loved to collect rare works of art. They had everything in their collection, from Picasso to Raphael. They would often sit together and admire the great works of art.

When the Vietnam conflict broke out, the son went to war. He was very courageous and died in battle while rescuing another soldier. The father was notified and grieved deeply for his only son.

About a month later, just before Christmas, there was a knock at the door. A young man stood at the door with a large package in his hands. He said, "Sir, you don't know me, but I am the soldier for whom your son gave his life. He saved many lives that day, and he was carrying me to safety when a bullet struck him in the heart and he died instantly. He often talked about you, and your love for art."

The young man held out his package. "I know this isn't much. I'm not really a great artist, but I think your son would have wanted you to have this."

The father opened the package. It was a portrait of his son, painted by the young man. He stared in awe at the way the soldier had captured the personality of his son in the painting. The father was so drawn to the eyes that his own eyes welled up with tears. He thanked the young man and offered to pay him for the picture.

"Oh, no sir, I could never repay what your son did for me. It's a gift."

The father hung the portrait over his mantle. Every time visitors came to his home, he took them to see the portrait of his son before he showed them any of the other great works he had collected. The man died a few months later. There was to be a great auction of his paintings. Many influential people gathered, excited over seeing the great paintings and having an opportunity to purchase one for their collection. On the platform sat the painting of the son.

The auctioneer pounded his gavel. "We will start the bidding with this picture of the son. Who will bid for this picture?"

There was silence. Then a voice in the back of the room shouted, "We want to see the famous paintings. Skip this one."

But the auctioneer persisted, "Will someone bid for this painting? Who will start the bidding? $100, $200?"

Another voice shouted angrily, "We didn't come to see this painting. We came to see the Van Gogh's, the Rembrandts. Get on with the real bids!"

But still the auctioneer continued, "The son! The son! Who'll take the son?"

Finally, a voice came from the very back of the room. It was the longtime gardener of the man and his son. "I'll give $10 for the painting." Being a poor man, it was all he could afford.

"We have $10, who will bid $20?"

"Give it to him for $10. Let's see the masters."

"$10 is the bid, won't someone bid $20?"

The crowd was becoming angry. They didn't want the picture of the son. They wanted the more worthy investments for their collections. The auctioneer pounded the gavel.

"Going once, twice, SOLD for $10!"

A man sitting on the second row shouted, "Now let's get on with the collection!"

The auctioneer laid down his gavel, "I'm sorry, the auction is over."

"What about the paintings?"

"I am sorry. When I was called to conduct this auction, I was told of a secret stipulation in the will. I was not allowed to reveal that stipulation until this time. Only the painting of the son would be auctioned. Whoever bought that painting would inherit the entire estate, including the paintings. The man who took the son gets everything!"[6]

I've read this story a hundred times, and every time I feel a tear of gratitude because I know the reality that when I took the Son, I got it all. And you did too. If you search for this story on Snopes.com, you will discover it is technically just a story, but it nevertheless makes a profound point: When you have Jesus, you have everything in *Father*'s estate.

When Jay-Z and Beyoncé had their daughter Blue Ivy, he wrote the song, "Glory," in which he sings about having a child from the child of Destiny's Child.[7] Their ten-day-old infant was perhaps the youngest person in history to ever have a song in the charts. The coolest thing is that you, too, are destiny's child, and so am I. You and I are *Abba*'s child.

Now that you are reborn, you are a full-fledged adopted son or daughter. *Father* loves you and He wants you to know that you belong. Along with brushing your teeth and combing your hair, it is a good idea to incorporate this prayer into your daily routine:

Father, re-parent me in Jesus' name.

7

Father's Child

WHEN YOU ARE *Abba's* child, you are given a new heart. Your spirit is re-born and with your new heart you literally become a new person. *Father* describes it this way: "If anyone is in Christ, he is a new creation. The old has passed away; behold, the new has come" (2 Cor. 5:17).

The key to making the transition from orphan to daughter or son is learning to live out of your new heart and your new identity; but first, you need to remove the orphan spirit and orphan mentality. This can be a challenging transition. When you spend the better part of your life living like a street-kid, bag-lady, or beggar, the orphan habits are difficult to kick. Jack Frost put his finger on something profound. "Left unchecked, an orphan heart can grow into a stronghold of oppression—a habit structure of thinking or fortress of thought that is so deeply entrenched that only a profound experiential revelation of *Father* God's love can displace it."[1]

As we saw in the Romanian orphan crisis, reactive attachment disorder (RAD) is the result of neglect, abuse, or abrupt separation from caregivers from infancy to three years. When infants and small children are denied love, alienated for extended times, or shuffled between caregivers, they are taught to be untrusting, insecure, and distant. Their ability to receive love, comfort, and affection can be permanently damaged. Interpersonal behavioral skills can be crippled, and the long-term effects are disastrous. Children become impulsive, controlling, manipulative, cold, distant and angry. Eating disorders, depression, self-hatred, and sexual brokenness often result.

Such children have a tendency to mutilate pets, harm siblings, and damage themselves. Dozens of articles on RAD patients have been written by Mayo Clinic and virtually every other medical institution.[2]

At the heart of RAD is an inability to love and to be loved. While you and I most likely do not suffer the extreme symptoms of RAD, we have all experienced a degree of damage to our love receptors, and we need healing.

White Noise

As we have seen, Satan is a liar and the father of the orphan heart and the orphan spirit. He is constantly lying to you. The orphan spirit sits on your shoulder like a bird and whispers lies into your ear. While the orphan spirit cannot make you an orphan, it can certainly make you feel like one. He lies to you about your body, your abilities, your relationships, your sexuality, your future, your worth, and even about your adoption. Most likely you have heard some of these thoughts. Perhaps they have crawled across your brain so many times they have dug a ditch.

The orphan spirit lies about your body and abilities.

> *You are ugly.*
> *You are stupid.*

It lies about your relationships.

> *You are all alone.*
> *No one loves you.*
> *You are abandoned—rejected.*
> *You don't belong here.*

It lies about your sexuality.

> *You are not who you think you are.*
> *You are sexually confused.*
> *The gender on your birth certificate is backwards.*
> *You are queer.*

It lies about your future.

> *You will never succeed.*
> *You are a loser.*
> *Your life is hopeless.*
> *You would be better off dead.*
> *You are a piece of trash.*

It lies about your adoption as *Abba's* child.

> *God doesn't hear your prayers.*
> *God doesn't love you.*
> *If God loved you, this would never have happened.*
> *You have fallen and you can't get up.*
> *God was absent when you were abused.*
> *You deserve better.*
> *Curse God and die.*

The orphan spirit is actually a religious spirit, which means that it thrives in prayer environments—churches, mosques, temples, synagogues, cathedrals, tabernacles and even in your own private prayer time. The orphan spirit tries to hijack your *Father*-time and render it useless. If your *Father*-time makes you anxious, agitated, or fearful, you can be sure the orphan spirit has taken over.

Now that you are a legally adopted child of *Father* God, with all rights and privileges, He wants to remove the orphan spirit and the orphan mentality that comes with it. It may be helpful to consider the orphan spirit in contrast to the Spirit of adoption.

<u>Orphan Spirit</u>	<u>Spirit of Adoption</u>
Rejection	Acceptance
Distrust	Trust
Abandonment	Belonging
Loneliness	Companionship
Anxiety/fear	Love/freedom
Hopeless	Hopeful
Poverty	Abundance
Hurts/wounds/pain	Healing
Abuse	Respect
Dishonor	Honor
Curses	Blessings
Insecurity	Security
Fear of Death	Assurance of Salvation
Wandering	Home

These two spirits have been in conflict throughout human history—the orphan spirit and the Spirit of sonship. The Spirit of adoption has no greater enemy than the orphan spirit—the two are in conflict with each other because they both want to control your heart and mind. Now that you are *Abba*'s child, you have authority over the orphan spirit.

In order to enjoy the benefits of being *Abba's* child, you can silence the white noise of other voices, particularly the voice of the orphan spirit. You don't need to just passively sit there and allow the Enemy to smack you in the face with his lies like a punching bag. Now that you are adopted, you want to take dominion over your mind and your thought process. You can say, "No" to the lies and you can put an end to the tormenting voices of the orphan spirit.

> **Exercise your authority as Abba's child and break off that insidious orphan spirit.**

The orphan spirit is an imposter; the Spirit of adoption is the genuine, and is more powerful. *Father's* loving Spirit of adoption is actually the most powerful force in the universe—it is stronger than anything you will ever face.

Right now, you can exercise your authority as *Abba's* child and break off that insidious orphan spirit. The following declaration is a good one. It has been field-tested in the trenches all over the world, and I present it to you now. Not to put words in your mouth, but if you are sick and tired of being treated like a spirit-orphan, and you want to silence the lies, this declaration may help you express what's inside your heart:

> I am *Abba's* child through *Abba's* Son, Jesus. I am legally adopted with all rights and privileges, and I gladly come under *Abba's* authority. In *Abba's* authority, I now take authority over the orphan spirit. I bind you, orphan spirit, in the name of the Lord Jesus Christ, and I command you to be gone from me now, for it is written, "Resist the devil, and he will flee from you" (James 4:7). I break you off from

me; I am free from you now and forever. Be gone and never again return to me in the name of the Lord Jesus Christ.

I further declare, as *Abba*'s child, that I am legally adopted, forever loved, accepted, protected, and blessed.

Congratulations! If you were able to make this declaration, you are now free in Jesus' name!

The Bible is written to help you transition from an orphan mentality to begin seeing yourself as *Abba*'s child. The entire book of Psalms is a book that connects every thought and emotion to *Father*. The entire book of Proverbs helps you leave the foolishness of the orphan mentality and to live as a full-fledged, wisdom-seeker.

There is no better way to express the Spirit of adoption, which is the Spirit of Jesus, than to forgive those who have hurt you. Jack Frost gives eight action steps that you may find helpful in transforming your mind from orphan thinking to adoption thinking:

1. Forgive your parents for misrepresenting *Father*'s love to you.

2. Ask your parents to forgive you for the way you hurt or disappointed them.

3. Focus your life upon being a son or daughter of God.

4. Forgive spiritual and governmental authorities.

5. You may need to seek forgiveness from those in authority.

6. Daily renounce ungodly beliefs and hidden lies of orphan thinking.

7. Begin sowing into your inheritance.

8. Enter into your inheritance.[3]

When you are re-born, you receive a new self, and *Father* wants you to know your new self: "Put on the new self, which is being renewed in knowledge after the image of its creator" (Col. 3:10). One of the coolest parts of your new self is that you get a whole new set of motivations, and your passions and desires change from the inside. Things you used to enjoy will now seem like distractions, and things that used to seem boring will now become exciting. *Father* wants you to know, "It is God who works in you, both to will and to work for his good pleasure" (Phil. 2:13).

This new self with its new passions and motivations is what keeps you from ever feeling the need to fake it. Learning to live out of your new self with its new heart is the key to being *Abba's* child.

Childlikeness

The longer I follow *Father*, the more He reduces me to a child. I am not talking about being childish; I am talking about being childlike. Childlikeness is the mark of spirit maturity; childishness is the mark of immaturity. As you grow in an every-increasing love relationship with *Father*, you will become increasingly dependent on Him, delightfully playful, and certainly more spontaneous and serendipitous. Spurgeon helps clarify childlikeness:

> One work of the Holy Spirit is to create in believers the spirit of adoption. . . . We are regenerated by the Holy Spirit, and so receive the nature of children; and that nature, which is given by him, he continually prompts, and excites, and develops, and matures; so that we receive day by day more and more of the child-like spirit.[4]

Some people age prematurely. In the unusual 1996 film, *Jack*, starring Robin Williams, a fifth grade boy has curiously grown into a middle-aged man. As bizarre as the movie plot sounds, it all too clearly portrays a common reality; people become stiff, easily bored, increasingly brittle, pridefully pompous, ceremonially stodgy, predictably set in their ways, and arrogantly superior and entitled.

Jesus made sure that the belly-aching, religious sour-pusses of his day were identified as phonies. He said, "For you are like whitewashed tombs, which outwardly appear beautiful, but within are full of dead people's bones and all uncleanliness" (Matt. 23:27). When people lose touch with *Father*'s love and their own child-like heart, they become mean-spirited, angry, judgmental, and intolerant. Laws without love, doctrine without delight, and religious ritual without relationship, becomes toxic.

It's sad to discover how many people who have been going to church for years carry with them an aging orphan heart. Their religious robes became costumes that hide their bogus pretense. Their religious incense is like the disgusting lavender aerosol you spray in the bathroom after you release noxious gasses from your bowels.

Bottom line, it's not that these guys are any worse than the rest of us—they've just lost touch with *Father*. They do, however, stand as a marker, like a shrine with discolored, wilted flowers on the side of the highway that marks a ve-hicular death, the religious monuments of our past remind us all of the lethal highway of religion without relationship, of faith without *Father*. Dead religion is nothing but form without fullness, legalism without love, a mask without a face, and an orphan without a heart.

The joy of being *Abba's* child is the fact that you get continually younger—your body may age, but your spirit is being rejuvenated. *Father* reverses your aging process. You don't need the fountain of youth. You don't need the latest skin cream. What you need is to be re-parented. As a papa who loves his grandchildren, there is nothing I enjoy more than to hear them say with a grin bigger than their face, "Again! Papa, again! Do it again!" If it was fun to climb on my neck once, it's even more fun doing it twenty times. As you are re-parented, you will love singing the same worship song over and over and over again. You will never get tired of prayer, worship, Bible reading, fellowship with the family. Again, *Father.* Let's do it again! And again.

It may be helpful to show the contrast between what it is to be childish and what it is to be childlike.

Childish	Childlike
Foolish	Playful
Irresponsible	Spontaneous
Immature	Flexible
Reckless	Easily Surprised
Careless	Dependent
Pouting	Praising
Demanding	Grateful
Entitled	Thankful

This is not some petty distinction, this is the essence of spiritual maturity. The more you mature in Christ, the less childish you become and the more childlike you become. When Jesus said, "Let the little children come to me . . . for such is the kingdom of heaven" (Matt. 19:14), He wasn't talking strictly about those less than twenty-one years of age—He was talking to you, too. Brennon Manning thought Jesus was on to something: "Unless we reclaim our child, we will have no inner sense of self."[5]

Re-parenting reverses the aging process. The longer we walk with *Father* God, the younger we get. The key to the kingdom is to become childlike. Re-parenting starts the moment we are born again, and it continues through all eternity. Frederick Buechner adds:

> We are children, perhaps at the very moment when we know that it is as children that God loves us—not because we have deserved his love and not in spite of our undeserving; not because we try and not because we recognize the futility of our trying; but simply because he has chosen to love us. We are children because he is our father; and all our efforts, fruitful and fruitless, to do good, to speak truth, to understand, are the efforts of children who, for all their precocity, are children still in that before we loved him, he loved us, as children, through Jesus Christ our Lord.[6]

The Spirit of adoption that now lives inside you wants to be re-parented—it craves an ever-deepening love-relationship with *Dad*. As *Abba*'s child, there may be no more appropriate way for you to express your trust in Him than to pray this prayer:

Father, re-parent me in Jesus' name.

8

Father's Love

THE GREATEST FORCE on earth is *Father*'s love, and until you recognize it as such, you are only dabbling. When *Father*'s love means something to you, it means everything.

Every orphan has been damaged physically, mentally, emotionally and relationally, which means their love receptors have been damaged. Orphans have learned by experience that people are not to be trusted.

Your hand is full of touch receptors, but if the nerves that run up your arm are severed, the receptors are ineffective. The inside of your eyeball is covered with light receptors, but no matter how well these receptors work, if the optic nerve is cut, you are blind. Your mouth is full of taste buds, but if your dentist injects Novocain into your cheek in order to remove a cavity, you can taste nothing.

In the same way, your heart is full of love receptors that are damaged and require healing and activation in order for you to receive the *Father*'s love. Damage to your love receptors is what psychologists call reactive attachment disorder (RAD). The same *Father* who healed the lepers, opened blind eyes, and raised the dead is now wanting to heal your love receptors, and at the same time, heal you from RAD. As *Abba*'s child, you have access to the healing of *Abba*'s Son.

Love Receptors

The healing of your love receptors is where *Abba*'s healing begins. *Father* wants you to know love by experience, and healing your love receptors is what makes it possible. All emotional healing is connected to the healing of your love receptors, and until you receive healing of your love receptors, love will always remain an abstract theory and not an experience. Healing your love receptors is where re-parenting begins as well.

Abba has been healing my love receptors for many years, and I have seen him heal the love receptors of literally millions of spiritual orphans around the world. No exaggeration. If I had not experienced this healing in my own soul, and had not seen it firsthand in countless others, I would not be writing with the same degree of certainty. *Father* starts the internal transformation of your life by healing your love receptors.

It is helpful to affirm the reality of *Father*'s love. There is healing power in the declaration of truth, and this declaration is designed to initiate the healing of your love receptors. While it is not a silver bullet that guarantees full emotional healing, it is most certainly a big step in the right direction. While I encourage you to continue to seek *Father* for full healing, this declaration is worth making now. And as you do, I encourage you to open both hands—open them wide with your palms facing up as if you are receiving a gift. Prop your book open, if need be, so it will stay open on its own. This declaration contains a big ask, and you want to be in a posture to receive.

I am *Abba's* child. I am loved, blessed, and highly favored. I used to be an orphan—I was wounded, lied to, cursed and broken. I was damaged goods, but today I bring my wounds into the open; I have no need to hide. I am adopted, accepted and loved. I am *Abba's* child, and I will never again be rejected.

I confess to You my anger, resentment, and unforgiveness. I put my damaged emotions under the blood of Your Son, and I now receive the antiseptic cleansing of Your love. I specifically renounce the spirit of bitterness in the name of the Lord Jesus Christ—take it from me now and forever. I open to You my heart and ask You to heal my love receptors. You have given me a new heart; heal my father-wounds. I want You to heal all my reactive attachment disorder and my orphan issues and heal my love receptors. From this day forward, I anticipate Your on-going healing as I spend time in Your presence.

Don't allow the brevity of this declaration to let you question the reality of your healing. *Father* is a wonderful counselor and He will certainly give you fuller insight into your healing process in the days to come, but His healing is often quick and painless.

Love Infusion

Now that *Father* is healing your love receptors, He doesn't simply want you to take a little sip of His love. He doesn't want to simply sprinkle a few drops on your tongue from an eyedropper. He wants you to take the plunge and jump head-first into the depths of His love, and He wants to literally immerse, saturate, and fill you to overflowing with His love.

This love-infusion is a big deal. It's what is called "the promise of the *Father*" and it's so dynamic that Jesus even compared it to water baptism by immersion: "He ordered them . . . to wait for the promise of the *Father*, which, he said, 'you heard from me; for John baptized with water, but you will be baptized with the Holy Spirit'" (Acts 1:4–5).

It's important to insert a few sidebar observations at this point about the Holy Spirit. We have looked at *Father*'s Son, but I want to introduce you to the third person in *Father*'s immediate family—His Spirit.

> ## THE HOLY SPIRIT IS JUST AS MUCH A PERSON AS GOD THE *FATHER* AND GOD THE SON.

The Spirit of God is sometimes regarded as the forgotten person. Though frequently compared to inanimate objects like fire, wind, water, or oil, the Holy Spirit is just as much a person as God the *Father* and God the Son. He has feelings and can grieve like a person.[1] He has a will and gives gifts like a person.[2] He has a mind and thinks like a person.[3] R.A. Torrey understood the personhood of the Spirit: "It is impos-3sible to rightly understand the work of the Holy Spirit, or to get into right relation with the Holy Spirit Himself and thus know His blessed work in our souls, without first coming to know the Holy Spirit is a Person."[4]

The Spirit is a loving, praying, freeing Spirit, and His primary role is to draw attention to Jesus: "He will bear witness about me" (John 15:26), and, "He will glorify me" (16:14), Jesus said.

The same Spirit that gave you re-birth is the Spirit who now wants to baptize you, or saturate you, with His loving presence. When you are baptized in the Spirit, you are energized on a whole new level. While your position as daughter or son will not change, your experience and appreciation certainly will change. *Father*'s Book says it this way: "God's love has been poured out [*exkeo*] into our hearts through the Holy Spirit who has been given to us" (Rom. 5:5).

Exkeo means to recklessly spill or gush out, and *Father* wants His love to recklessly spill and gush out into you. *Father* wants to baptize you in the water of His Spirit, not from a little garden hose, but from His own personal fire hydrant.

John Wesley's friend Howell Harris documented in his diary the impact of the promise of the *Father* in his own life.

> June 18, 1735. Being in secret prayer I felt suddenly my heart melting within me like wax before a fire, with love to God my Saviour. I felt not only love and peace, but also a longing to be dissolved and to be totally unacquainted before, it was this—'Abba, Father; Abba, Father'. I could not help calling God my Father: I knew that I was his child, and that he loved ; my soul being filled and satiated, crying, 'It is enough—I am satisfied; give me strength and I will follow thee through fire and water, springing up into everlasting life', yea, the love of God was shed abroad in my heart by the Holy Ghost.[5]

You cannot force an egg to hatch, or a flower to open, and you cannot rush the process of re-parenting, but *Father* has a way of creating environments that are conducive to growth, and He can rapidly change the environment around your heart in a hurry. When Jesus stood up in the middle of tens of thousands of worshippers, He instantly changed the entire atmosphere when He said at the top of his lungs, "If anyone thirsts, let him come to me and drink" (John 7:37).

Among that mass of people who were all outward worshippers, *Father* was looking for people who were heart-worshippers and hungry. He even went on to promise, "Out of his heart will flow rivers of living water" (7:38). These rivers are Holy Spirit rivers that flow from the heart, or spirit, of people who are ready and hungry.

What about you? Are you ready and hungry? Has God put inside your spirit a love and thirst for the loving infusion of the Holy Spirit? If not, wait; if so, I submit to you this declaration. Just as you receive your adoption by faith, you receive the infusion of the Holy Spirit by faith. I want to encourage you to read this declaration before you pray it; you want to pray it thoughtfully:

> *Father*, I put myself before You as Your child. I am not perfect, but I am reborn and adopted. I am accepted in Christ and I will never be rejected. I am protected in Christ and I have nothing to fear. I am blessed in Christ and my life is significant. Your Word tells me, "be filled with the Spirit" (Eph. 5:18), and it promises me, "You will be baptized with the Holy Spirit" (Acts 1:5). So right now, *Father*, I receive the infilling and the infusion of the Holy Spirit in the name of the Lord Jesus Christ. Fill every area of my life, saturate me—spirit, soul, and body—with Your presence. Take control of my mind, will, and emotions, and fill every part of my body. Flood me now with your love. I receive Your fullness in the name of the Lord Jesus Christ.

Now that you have read the declaration, if it expresses what your heart desires, I encourage you to waste no time. Open your hands, open your heart, re-read the declaration, and receive.

All In

It's time to take a knee. We kneel in the presence of greatness, and there is nothing greater than *Father*'s love. When the apostle Paul encountered *Father*'s love, he took a knee:

"For this reason I bow my knees before the *Father*" (Eph. 3:14). He went on to describe the vastness of *Father's* four-dimensional love—breadth, length, height, and depth.

> That you, being rooted and grounded in love, may have strength to comprehend with all the saints what is the breadth and length and height and depth, and to know the love of Christ that surpasses knowledge, that you may be filled with all the fullness of God. (3:17–19)

Each of these dimensions is worth a closer look.

The *breadth* of *Father's* love shows that He is all-inclusive. *Father's* love is so wide that it includes all nations, all ages, all people—it even includes me and you. If you have tried to run away from *Father's* love, or are living on the fringe, or have tried your best to reject His love, *Father* wants you to know His love is wider still.

Length represents *Father's* inexhaustible love—that He will go to any length to love you. It is breathtaking to consider *Father's* love will never end—it will never run out, never quit, never give up—not on you, not on me, not on anyone.

Height represents how insurmountable *Father's* love is. No principle in philosophy, no problem in physics, no theorem in mathematics is higher than *Father's* love. No matter how high you climb the latter of success, or how high you get in your profession, or how high you run up your credit card debt, or how high you pile your garbage, *Father's* love is higher still.

Depth represents *Father's* humility—His willingness to stoop to anything to reach you. *Father's* love is deeper than the ditch you fall into, deeper than the pig's pen, deeper than the gutter, deeper than your debt, deeper than your depression, misery, self-hatred, or despair. As my pastor friend told me following the suicide of his twenty-one-year-old son,

"My wife and I have been to the absolute bottom of depression and despair, lower than we ever dreamed possible, and I have discovered one thing—when you hit bottom, *Father* is right there next to you." You can't run away from God's love. You can't wear out God's love. You can't climb over it, and you can't crawl under it.

Fredrick Lehman was at a place of desperation. He lost his business and all his material possessions and was forced to work long days of manual labor in a packing house. One Sunday, despite his circumstances, he was so moved by *Father*'s love, he couldn't sleep and began jotting down lyrics on scraps of paper. A melody came quickly, followed by the lyrics:

> The love of God is greater far
>> Than tongue or pen can ever tell
> It goes beyond the highest star
>> And reaches to the lowest hell
> The guilty pair, bowed down with care
>> God gave His Son to win
> His erring child He reconciled
>> And pardoned from his sin
>
> O love of God, how rich and pure!
>> How measureless and strong!
> It shall forevermore endure
>> The saints' and angels' song.

While his lyrics only contained two verses, he knew in those days that songs were expected to have three verses. It was then he discovered words that had been transcribed from the inside of a prison cell wall, where some incarcerated soul wrote down word-for-word the lyrics we now know as the final verse of one of history's most beloved hymns, "The Love of God." It turned out that those words were written from memory, because they date back to a Hebrew verse written by a Jewish Rabbi a thousand years earlier.

> Could we with ink the ocean fill
> > And were the skies of parchment made
> Were every stalk on earth a quill
> > And every man a scribe by trade
> To write the love of God above
> > Would drain the ocean dry
> Nor could the scroll contain the whole
> > Though stretched from sky to sky.[6]

Our Battle Cry

Don't think for a moment that *Father's* love is wimpy, soft, anemic, impractical, sentimental, wishy-washy, or irrelevant. *Father's* love is the greatest force on earth.

The worst day of my life was the day that our precious daughter, Andrea, was diagnosed with cancer—a rapidly growing, inoperable, large B-cell lymphoma. It had grown undetected in her chest cavity around her heart, and we learned that it had already broken a rib.

When Sherry and I received the news, we held each other and screamed. Within ten minutes, Sherry and I told *Father* two things: "We will praise you no matter what happens, and we will keep our hearts in your love." *Father's* love for us and for our daughter was not up for grabs—He had already proven His love for us on the cross. He did not need to heal Andrea in order to prove His love for us. That fact was settled.

Though we would never stop asking for Andrea's healing, we resolved that no matter what happened, we would also keep praising. God was praiseworthy, and we would praise Him regardless.

During this time, God gave us a battle cry. When the journey got tough, we would declare over our daughter and over her cancer, "Give thanks to the LORD . . . for his steadfast love endures forever" (Ps. 106:1).

This is the same declaration that God gave ancient Israel when they were surrounded by hostile armies. When they needed a breakthrough, God gave them a most counterintuitive strategy: instead of soldiers, send out singers; instead of you fighting this battle, the Lord will fight for you; rather than calling on God for His wrath against your enemies, simply declare the love of *Father*; rather than your own playlist, sing this single lyric, and sing it repetitively over and over and over again, all day long: "Give thanks to the LORD . . . for his steadfast love endures forever."

Israel obeyed. They sang. None of the soldiers lifted a finger. God fought. Their enemies turned against each other and killed each other. When the war was over, all God's children needed to do was go out on the battlefield and pick up the spoils of war, and that day God's children got rich off their enemies.

In our daughter's battle, the next ten months were brutal. We made dozens of trips from Atlanta to Dallas where Andrea was being treated. Our precious daughter received 600 hours of chemotherapy, which radically shrunk her tumor. When the surgeon went in to remove what they thought was a walnut-sized tumor, however, it turned out to be the size of a large grapefruit.

The surgery, scheduled for forty-five minutes, lasted more than three hours. When she came out of the operating room, she seemed to have tubes coming from everywhere. It was a long recovery followed by six weeks of radiation. It was exhausting, but during the entire time, we never stopped praising, and we never stopped receiving *Father's* love. Eleven months later, she was declared cancer-free. That was eight years ago.

Our only daughter already had four daughters of her own, but a year later she learned she was pregnant. She called her oncologist with concerns, "Is the baby going to be okay? Am I going to be okay?" Her doctor assured her that she should be fine. When the baby was born, after having four girls, God gave her a son, Josiah James Smith. *Father* did not need to do that for us to prove His love, nor to deserve our praise. But He did, and we give Him the credit.

WILL YOU GIVE PRAISE TO *FATHER*? WILL YOU KEEP YOUR HEART IN HIS LOVE?

You may be facing a battle of your own right now—and you need a battle cry. As counterintuitive as it sounds, every day you get out of bed, the two greatest battles you face are (1) Will you give praise to *Father*? and (2) Will you keep your heart in His love? This war-cry is designed to enable you to win both battles. If you win these two battles, you can win every other battle you face. And if you do not win these battles, every other battle you face will be that much more difficult.

Our family miracle reminds me of another family miracle. Just a few days before Christmas in 2017, Joel and Janie Taylor's two-year-old son Jackson became ill and had to go to the ER. They soon learned that the boy had hemolytic-uremic syndrome or HUS. They hadn't slept for weeks. Their friends rallied in prayer.

When their good friends Jonathan and Melissa Hesler got word that it was unlikely Jackson would live through the night, Jonathan suddenly discerned that a giant spirit of unbelief was their biggest enemy and a melody immediately erupted in his heart. He began to write the song, "Raise a Hallelujah," which has now become a crazy popular Bethel praise song. It talks about raising a hallelujah in the presence of enemies and when facing unbelief, because hallelujah is a weapon, and hallelujah recognizes that God Himself fights our battles.[7]

Jonathan sent this song to Joel, who listened to it repeatedly and played it to his son, who was fighting for his life. Soon after New Year, Jackson finally started to improve and never had another relapse.

On January 16, 2018, the Taylor family went home from the hospital. It had been one month since Jackson had been outside. Janie said, "This is part of our story now, and it is part of Jackson's testimony of his life, that the world will know that miracles happen."[8]

In an Instagram post December 30, 2017, Joel wrote, "Thank you, Global church, for your prayers and support. You've been our lifeline more than you can imagine. You held our arms up when we have no more strength."[9] You can do a web search for their names now and watch the parents tell their own story on YouTube.

Today you can raise a hallelujah! You can use your war-cry to stand your ground against the enemies around you. You might as well face it—learning to be *Abba*'s child means learning to pray. And there is no better place to start than here and there is no better time than now:

Father, re-parent me in Jesus' name.

9

Father's Ear

*F*ATHER IS A GOOD listener. He wants you to know you have a voice—your voice matters, and He wants you to use it. *Father* says, "Everyone who calls upon the name of the Lord shall be saved" (Acts 2:21). Having 24/7 access to *Father's* ear is a big deal.

When Jesus' disciples presented Him with a simple five-word request, "Lord, teach us to pray" (Luke 11:1), Jesus immediately gave them a straightforward, five-word answer, "When you pray, say: *Father*, . . ." (Luke 11:2).

The five most radical words Jesus ever said may be, "When you pray, say: *Father*." He might as well have barged into Caesars Palace in Las Vegas, grabbed the craps tables in his bare hands, and flipped them upside down. That day, He certainly turned religion on its ear.

To some, it would have sounded disrespectful, simplistic, shallow, unsophisticated, childish! But Jesus did not come to babysit the religious bullies; He came to adopt orphans like you and me. The fact is, *Father* gave us His Son so that He might give us His ear.

Listening

Many dads wish they had spent more time with their kids when they had the chance, and looking back, many kids wish the same. When Harry Chapin wrote "Cat's in the Cradle," he put his finger on an emotionally super-charged issue: that most dads are lousy talkers, and most kids are lousy listeners. The pungent lyrics follow the timeline of a typical dad who misses every stage of his child's development until it's too late. When his son is grown and the dad finally calls, the son says he'd love to get together, if he could only find the time. The chorus that constantly loops throughout the song expresses the tragedy of wishful thinking and empty promises as if to say, "Sure, dad, we'll have a good time when we get around to it—not!"[1] If Harry Chapin had a penny for every tear cried during this song, he would be the richest man in the world.

You may have regrets over neglected family relationships, but you now have a Dad who knows how to listen, and He has all the time in the world. If you are a beginner in prayer, *Father* is your starting point; if you have years of experience in prayer, you will never go any further than *Father*. He is the start line and the finish line. He strips away all the religious wrappings and trappings, and reduces prayer to a love relationship.

The Ocean

As we said earlier, if prayer is an ocean, *Father* is the shallow entry point where you initiate your relationship; *Father* is also the Mariana Trench where you go deep. The idea of comparing prayer to an ocean is not original to me. Habakkuk prophesied 2700 years ago, "The earth will be filled with the knowledge of the glory of the LORD as the waters cover the sea" (Hab. 2:14). The prophet could see the day when prayer would cover the earth, and Orphans R Us would become *Father's* house. While only 71% of the earth's surface is currently covered with water, on that day, 100% of the earth's surface will be covered by the knowledge of the glory of the Lord.

Scientists tell us that if the water in all the oceans were measured it would be equivalent to 321 million cubic miles of water. To put that in perspective, since we normally calibrate water in reference to gallons, just one cubic mile contains more than 1.1 trillion gallons of water. Allow me to restate my thesis: if the oceans of the world were prayer, and one day they most certainly will be, every drop in every ocean would be the love of *Father*. We are not talking about a few drops, we are talking about 1.1 trillion gallons in every one of the 321 million cubic miles of ocean.[2] If you are *Abba's* child, that should at least make you smile.

According to the National Ocean Service, there is only one global ocean, just as there is only one God, and most oceanographers currently recognize five ocean basins—the Atlantic, Pacific, Indian, Arctic, and Southern (Antarctic) Oceans. These five ocean basins correspond to the five primary bodies of prayer—worship, lordship, sonship, fellowship, and leadership.[3] And they all form a single ocean of loving relationship with *Father*.

The average ocean depth is 12,451 feet, which sounds crazy deep to me, since where I snorkel in the Bahamas averages a modest 33 feet. Located in the Western Pacific Ocean about two kilometers from the Mariana Islands, is the deepest trench on earth. The Mariana Trench is shaped like a smile and measures about 2,550 km in length and 69 km wide and plunges almost three times the average depth.

On the southern end of the smile is a small slot shaped valley in the trench known as Challenger Deep, and it has officially been measured at 10,984 meters, or 36,037 feet, or almost seven miles deep. To give this perspective, if you could hypothetically put Mount Everest into the trench, it would still be under the water by more than 1.2 miles, or two kilometers.

> **NO MATTER HOW WELL YOU KNOW** *FATHER*, **YOU WILL NEVER EXHAUST HIS DEPTHS.**

There has never been a person—not a submarine, nor a drone—to ever come near the bottom of the trench; it has only been surveyed by echo sounding. It is fascinating that virtually every time drone submarines are sent to explore the trench, they return with soundings from even greater depths. And yes, there is life at that depth—creatures that defy science, sea life never seen anywhere else—but that's another story. While a few thousand people have climbed to the summit of Everest, only three people have ever dared to dive inside the trench, and none, not even a robotic submarine, has ever been to the bottom. Allow me to point out the obvious—no matter how well you know *Father*, you will never exhaust His depths. He will always exceed your experience.

The Shallows

When you pray, calling God *Father* may feel awkward at first. I pray with a lot of people each week, and it always surprises me how many people still call him God. In Jesus' day, virtually everyone called him God, Lord, Almighty; no one, and I mean no one, called him *Father*, that is, until Jesus came along. I always coach people to call Him *Father*; Jesus did, and I do too. Just think how significant a difference this makes. The name God is formal, distant, impersonal, generic. The name *Father* is personal, familial, relational, specific. *Father* clearly represents the kind of love relationship He wants with you.

I have a confession to make: I used to think that saying *Abba! Father!* was childish. It felt immature, awkward. I was convinced I had moved beyond such infantile prayer. Even writing these words brings to mind the arrogance, haughtiness, and pride of my heart—it makes me cry like a baby. Tears fill my eyes right now so that I can barely see straight. *Father* lovingly rebuked me last year by showing me that I will never outgrow the privilege of calling Him *Daddy*.

Though we have included this verse a few times already, it is worth another look: "For you did not receive the spirit of slavery to fall back into fear, but you have received the Spirit of adoption as sons, by whom we cry, '*Abba! Father!*'" (Rom. 8:15). Notice it does not say, by whom we cried, but rather, by whom we cry, *Abba! Father!* We don't simply cry *Abba! Father!* when we are first re-born; we continue to cry *Abba! Father! Daddy!* We never stop crying *Abba! Father!*—not today, not tomorrow, not ever. Sure, *Father* is the shallow zero entry into the ocean of His love, but *Father* is also the Mariana Trench.

The Deep

When you snorkel or scuba dive, the primary difference between the ocean depths and the shallows is getting in over your head. When your feet can no longer touch bottom and you are surrounded by water on all sides, you are no longer in control. The experience is both intimidating and exhilarating. Similarly, being surrounded on all sides by *Father*'s love is at the same time intimidating and exhilarating, because you are no longer in control, and that's the point. *Father* wants to break off from you and me the spirit of control. The deeper you go into *Father*'s love, the more you learn to trust Him, and the more you relinquish control.

Learning to snorkel and scuba dive came easy for me. From the gorgeous reefs of the Florida Keys to the endless coves of the Bahamas, I grew up with ample opportunities to enjoy the whole new world of ocean life. To this day, snorkeling remains one of my all-time favorite hobbies. Diving opens up a whole new world of fish, sponges, squids, crabs, lobsters, eels, and florescent fish in every imaginable shape and size. Swimming with sharks the size of our boat that could snap me in half with a single crunch is a rush. Crushing a spiny sea urchin and watching the reef fish swarm for an unexpected breakfast, swimming side-by-side with a six-foot manta ray, playing catch-and-release with a feisty three-pound lobster, or spear-fishing Nassau grouper and hog-snapper, are still at the top of my favorite things to do. But I must admit, as wild and exhilarating as the ocean floor can be, it doesn't even come close to the wide-eyed wonder with which I swim with *Father*. The vastness of His domain is more fulfilling and more invigorating, more spell-binding and overwhelming than a thousand trips to the Great Barrier Reef.

By now you should realize that the ocean of prayer and *Father*'s ear is more about being with Him than it is about receiving from Him. *Father*'s ear is not the chrome slot in the vending machine of prayer where you insert your coin to buy a bag of junk food. If it becomes that, you have slipped into the gutter of consumer-prayer. *Father's* ear is the conduit to His heart. His ear is open because His heart is open. More than giving to you, He wants to be with you.

Receiving

Just because I enjoy snorkeling and scuba diving in the ocean, does not prohibit me from catching a few fish that I can take home and cook for dinner. Just because the ocean of prayer is primarily about being with *Father*, don't think for a moment it is inappropriate to ask and receive. No one was more emphatic about asking and receiving than Jesus. He said, "And I tell you, ask, and it will be given to you; seek, and you will find; knock, and it will be opened to you. For everyone who asks receives, and the one who seeks finds, and to the one who knocks it will be opened" (Luke 11:9–10).

When He explained this principle of ask and receive, He even used human dads as an illustration: "What father among you, if his son asks for a fish, will instead of a fish give him a serpent; or if he asks for an egg, will give him a scorpion?" (Luke 11:11–12). The priority of being with *Father* does not for a second erase the essential role of receiving in prayer. *Father's* ear is not only connected to His heart; *Father's* ear is also connected to His hand. *Father* thrives on lavishly giving good gifts to His children. *Father* expects you not simply to ask, He expects you to receive.

Since the maturity of your spirit is defined by your child-likeness, you should understand that children are completely dependent on gifts from their parents. While independence in the human family is a mark of maturity, independence from *Father* is the primary mark of immaturity. Dependence on *Father* is one of the primary marks of spiritual maturity—the greater your dependence on *Father*, the greater your maturity.

In the middle of the Son's manifesto, commonly known as the Sermon on the Mount, Jesus repeated this *Father* family principle of dependence in several memorable word pictures. Each of these examples show the dependence of a healthy childlike soul. Just consider for a moment this brief list of some of the most-quoted words in history—quoted for the past two thousand years by presidents and kings, poets, philosophers, and prophets. They all have one major factor in common: they each show that childlike dependence is the mark of spirit maturity.

> Look at the birds of the air: they neither sow nor reap nor gather into barns, and yet your heavenly *Father* feeds them. Are you not of more value than they? . . .
>
> And why are you anxious about clothing? Consider the lilies of the field, how they grow: they neither toil nor spin, yet I tell you, even Solomon in all his glory was not arrayed like one of these. But if God so clothes the grass of the field, which today is alive and tomorrow is thrown into the oven, will he not much more clothe you, O you of little faith?
>
> Therefore do not be anxious, saying, 'What shall we eat?' or 'What shall we drink?' or 'What shall we wear?' For the Gentiles seek after all these things, and your heavenly *Father* knows that you need them all. (Matt. 6:26, 28–32)

Warning

As you do a deep-dive into *Father*, this is not an excuse to deep-dive into your pride. *Father* is not your alter-ego, and knowing Him does not make you superior to anyone else. To genuinely explore the depths of *Father* is not something to put on your résumé or give you a sense of entitlement. No one will present you with a fancy diploma to hang on the wall because of your intimacy with your *Dad*. Any such recognition would certainly cheapen the pursuit, and discredit its authenticity. Ultimately the exploration of *Father* is not about you—it's about Him.

John, given the generic title "the Voice," and known simply as "the baptizer," took a deep-dive into *Father* and into His Son. He appropriately concluded, "He must increase but I must decrease" (John 3:30). He obviously understood the deeper-you-go-the-smaller-you-feel principle.

> **PRAYER ALWAYS TAKES US BACK TO JESUS'**
> **WORDS, "WHEN YOU PRAY, SAY:** *FATHER*."

Too many of us as Christian leaders have over-complicated prayer—for ourselves and for our people. To our discredit, we have handed people elaborate prayer systems, while Jesus succinctly handed us *Father*. We give our people dozens of spiritual disciplines, and Jesus gives us *Father*. Don't get me wrong—I am not disparaging all prayer tools, prayer systems, and spiritual disciplines; I am, however, taking us back to Jesus' words, "When you pray, say: *Father*."

Asking *Father* for stuff is a mark of childlikeness—the more you ask, the more childlike you are. The following story beautifully illustrates the simplicity of asking and the miraculous wonder of receiving dramatic answers to specific prayers. Dr. Helen Roseveare, a medical doctor, tells the true story of one such dramatic answer.

> One night, in Central Africa, I had worked hard to help a mother in the labor ward; but in spite of all that we could do, she died leaving us with a tiny, premature baby and a crying, two-year-old daughter.

We would have difficulty keeping the baby alive. We had no incubator. We had no electricity to run an incubator, and no special feeding facilities. Although we lived on the equator, nights were often chilly with treacherous drafts.

A student-midwife went for the box we had for such babies and for the cotton wool that the baby would be wrapped in. Another went to stoke up the fire and fill a hot water bottle. She came back shortly, in distress, to tell me that in filling the bottle, it had burst. Rubber perishes easily in tropical climates. "it is our last hot water bottle!" she exclaimed. As in the West, it is no good crying over spilled milk; so, in Central Africa it might be considered no good crying over a burst water bottle. They do not grow on trees, and there are no drugstores down forest pathways. "All right," I said, "Put the baby as near the fire as you safely can; sleep between the baby and the door to keep it free from drafts. Your job is to keep the baby warm."

The following noon, as I did most days, I went to have prayers with many of the orphanage children who chose to gather with me. I gave the youngsters various suggestions of things to pray about and told them about the tiny baby. I explained our problem about keeping the baby warm enough, mentioning the hot water bottle. The baby could so easily die if it got chilled. I also told them about the two-year-old sister, crying because her mother had died. During the prayer time, one ten-year-old girl, Ruth, prayed with the usual blunt consciousness of our African children. "Please, God," she prayed, "send us a water bottle. It'll be no good tomorrow, God, the baby'll be dead; so, please send it this afternoon." While I gasped inwardly at the audacity of the prayer, she added by way of corollary, " …And while You are about it, would You please send a dolly for the little girl so she'll know You really love her?" As often with children's prayers, I was put on the spot. Could I honestly say, "Amen?" I just did not believe that God could do this. Oh, yes, I know that He can do everything: The Bible says so, but there are limits, aren't there? The only way God could answer this particular prayer would be by sending a parcel from the homeland. I had been in Africa for almost four years at that time, and I had never, ever received a parcel from home. Anyway, if anyone did send a parcel, who would put in a hot water bottle? I lived on the equator!

Halfway through the afternoon, while I was teaching in the nurses' training school, a message was sent that there was a car at my front door. By the time that I reached home, the car had gone, but there, on the veranda, was a large twenty-two pound parcel! I felt tears pricking my eyes. I could not open the parcel alone; so, I sent for the orphanage children. Together we pulled off the string, carefully undoing each knot. We folded the paper, taking care not to tear it unduly.

Excitement was mounting. Some thirty or forty pairs of eyes were focused on the large cardboard box. From the top, I lifted out brightly colored, knitted jerseys. Eyes sparkled as I gave them out. Then, there were the knitted bandages for the leprosy patients, and the children began to look a little bored. Next, came a box of mixed raisins and sultanas—— that would make a nice batch of buns for the weekend.

As I put my hand in again, I felt the . . . could it really be? I grasped it, and pulled it out. Yes, "A brand-new rubber, hot water bottle!" I cried. I had not asked God to send it; I had not truly believed that He could. Ruth was in the front row of the children. She rushed forward, crying out, "If God has sent the bottle, He must have sent the dolly, too!" Rummaging down to the bottom of the box, she pulled out the small, beautifully dressed dolly. Her eyes shone: She had never doubted! Looking up at me, she asked, "Can I go over with you, Mummy, and give this dolly to that little girl, so she'll know that Jesus really loves her?"

That parcel had been on the way for five whole months, packed up by my former Sunday School class, whose leader had heard and obeyed God's prompting to send a hot water bottle, even to the equator. One of the girls had put in a dolly for an African child—five months earlier in answer to the believing prayer of a ten-year-old to bring it "That afternoon!"[4]

This story has *Father* written all over it. I get goosebumps when I think of the audacity of an African orphan child who knew that her Dad was big enough to not only send a hot water bottle to a newborn infant who lived at the equator on the precise day it was needed, but that He would include a dolly for her sister. I get tears when I think that even in the packing of the parcel, the most important item is normally put in first, and since the dolly was in the bottom, it would seem that the person who sent it wanted to make sure it was included. What a picture of *Father*'s heart and *Father*'s ear. You may call it coincidence, but I have discovered that the more I ask, the more "coincidences" I see.

Re-parenting is invited, never forced. *Father* comes when He is welcomed, and His ear is toward those who call on Him, so keep your *Father*-tone simple. Too many sincere seekers have ruined their prayer time by making it overly structured and regimented.

Since you have a *Father* who sends hot water bottles to newborns and dolly's to African orphan children, what would keep you from wanting Him to re-parent you? Now is the time to ask:

Father, re-parent me in Jesus' name.

10

Father's Voice

ATHER IS A TALKER. He not only gives you His ear, He gives you His voice. Just as every healthy relationship is a two-way street, a healthy relationship with *Father* not only involves speaking to Him, but also hearing from Him.

Father is self-revealing. No one pries their way into His presence, and no one forces Him to speak. *Father* is like a one-way mirror—He sees everything from His side of the mirror, but we see nothing, that is, until He turns the light on. When *Father* sovereignly chooses to turn the light on, we call it revelation.

Fortunately for us, *Father* loves to talk. No one is a better listener than *Father*, and no one is a better talker. In fact, we could say, He never stops talking. The one true God—*Father*, Son, Spirit—talks in perfect harmony; that is to say, whenever God speaks, all three Persons are involved. When *Father* speaks, the Word is sent, and the Spirit activates the Word. Without the Son, you will never hear *Father*, and without the Spirit, you will never hear the Son.

Two Miracles

As we consider hearing God, it is essential to understand two realities: No one on their own can hear God's voice; and everyone re-born has the capacity to hear God's voice. Your ability to hear *Father*'s voice is not a matter of reading the right books, saying the right prayers, listening to praise music, fasting, or any other spiritual discipline. Your ability to hear *Father*'s voice always requires two miracles: revelation and activation.

Revelation is a miracle of transmission and activation is a miracle of reception. Revelation is what God does within Himself to speak; activation is what God does in you to be able to hear. Until *Father* chooses to reveal Himself and activate your hearing, you might as well be waiting for your phone to ring without a SIM card or Wi-Fi. Without revelation, there is no Wi-Fi or transmission, and without activation, there is no SIM card or reception. Good news: *Father* loves to reveal Himself, and He loves to activate your ability to hear Him speak.

> **THE PRIMARY WAY** *FATHER* **CHOOSES TO SPEAK IS DIRECTLY TO YOUR SPIRIT.**

The three primary ways He chooses to speak, as we said earlier, is through His Son, through His written Word, the Bible, and through His people. However, *Father* is also highly creative, and He has unlimited means by which He can choose to reveal Himself. He can speak through visions, dreams, word pictures, billboards, bumper stickers, and a thousand other options. The primary way God speaks, however, is not to your physical ear, nor to your mind or emotions, but to your spirit. Remember, your human spirit is what is now re-born; in fact, it is the only part of your life that is now re-born. For this reason, God speaks directly to your spirit.

There is one verse in *Father's* book that answers the three primary questions we have about hearing *Father's* voice: *How does Father talk? How do we hear? What does He normally say?* Read this verse carefully: "The Spirit himself bears witness with our spirit that we are children of God" (Rom. 8:16). Let's consider each of these three foundational questions one at a time.

How does Father talk? This verse says, "The Spirit himself bears witness." This means that *Father* always speaks by His Spirit—always, no exceptions. While He has unlimited means by which to speak—through the Bible, people, circumstances, prayer, visions, dreams—He always, always, always, speaks by His Spirit. The Holy Spirit of God is the One who gives both revelation and activation—revelation of *Father* in the Son, and activation in us to be able to hear and understand.

How do we hear? This verse says, "The Spirit himself bears witness with our spirit." This means that we hear God's voice in our spirit. It is our spirit that is re-born the moment we are adopted as sons and daughters. *Father* is certainly capable of speaking audibly, but the normal way He chooses to speak is not to your physical ears but to your spirit.

As we have said, you and I are a spirit, a soul, and a body. The body is your physical self, and it contains the spirit and the soul. The soul is made up of your mind, will, and emotions. The deepest part, however, is your spirit, and this is the only part of your life that is now born anew.

For this reason, the spirit is where you hear from *Father*. You do not need to read a book on hearing God, you simply need to learn to listen to the voice of the Spirit in your spirit. God wants you to know that not only do you have two physical ears that extend from the sides of your head, you also have spirit ears, which, when activated, are fully capable of hearing *Father's* voice. You will discover that one word from God changes everything.

What does He normally say? These verses tell us that what *Father* continually says to you and me is that we are children of God. This means that He is constantly speaking to you related to your position as His daughters or sons. He tells you things like, *I love you; you are special to Me; I have wonderful plans for you. You are one-of-a-kind; I am proud of you.*

The Obvious

As you learn to hear *Father's* voice, it is important that you don't miss the obvious means by which He normally speaks—through *Father's* book, the Bible. The Bible is a supernatural book full of God's words, which means it's full of the Word, the Son. There is a tendency when you begin to hear *Father's* voice in your spirit to get so excited about His prophetic word that you neglect His written word. This is a pit that many *Father*-followers fall into.

Jesus was a Bible guy; that is, He not only loved the Bible, He was a life-long student of the Bible. The New Testament contains 1,800 verses that contain Jesus' words; 180 of them quote the Old Testament. One out of ten statements by Jesus were quotes or direct references to the Old Testament Scripture. It is no wonder Jesus said, "Do not think that I have come to abolish the Law or the

Prophets; I have not come to abolish them but to fulfill them" (Matt. 5:17).

Immediately prior to launching His public ministry, Jesus confronted the devil with the words, "Man shall not live by bread alone, but by every word that comes from the mouth of God" (Matthew 4:4). If Jesus was a Bible guy, obviously you and I also want to be Bible people.

If you love *Father*, you will love the Bible. The more you read, the more the Spirit will speak to your spirit. This is why the Bible is called, "The sword of the Spirit" (Eph. 6:17). Jesus actually rebuked the Bible students of his day because they completely missed the point: "You search the Scriptures because you think that in them you have eternal life; and it is they that bear witness about me" (John 5:39).

Reading the Bible is not some type of intellectual exercise in scholarship; it's part of your daily *Father*-time. After His resurrection, Jesus gave a world-class Bible study, showing how the entire Bible points to Him: "Beginning with Moses and all the Prophets, he interpreted to them in all the Scriptures the things concerning himself" (Luke 24:27). This means that Jesus is in virtually every book in the Old Testament as well as in the New Testament.

Following this Bible study, those in His audience said to each other, "Did not our hearts burn within us while he talked to us on the road, while he opened to us the Scriptures?" (Luke 24:32). Their hearts were burning because they were set on fire by the flame of activation. Burning hearts are loving hearts—hearts in love with *Father* and with His Son. The central reason why the best-selling book by a long shot every year is the Word of *Father* is because *Father* loves to talk and people love to hear.

Secrets

Father not only loves to speak, He loves to tell secrets. He knows how important secrets are in developing true friendship. Jesus brought His disciples into His confidence, and they became his secret-keeping friends. He said to them, "To you it has been given to know the secrets of the kingdom of God, but for others they are in parables, so that 'seeing they may not see, and hearing they may not understand'" (Luke 8:10).

Similarly, *Father* kept secrets with David: "The friendship of the LORD is for those who fear him, and he makes known to them his covenant" (Ps. 25:14). Even Moses said, "The secret things belong to the LORD our God, but the things that are revealed belong to us and to our children forever, that we may do all the words of this law" (Deut. 29:29).

> **IF YOUR PRAYER LIFE IS MORE PUBLIC THAN PRIVATE, YOU ARE IN TROUBLE.**

Father not only tells secrets; He wants to teach us to be secret-keepers with Him. This is a significant part of developing your love-relationship with Him. He wants you to keep secrets when you give significant sums of money to poor and needy people, so that He can reward you openly.[1] He wants you to keep secrets when you spend significant *Father*-time in prayer, so that He can reward you openly.[2] He wants you to keep secrets when you fast and skip meals, so that He can reward you openly.[3]

If your prayer life is more public than private, you are in trouble. A public prayer life that is better known among people on earth than it is by *Father* in heaven, is superficial and phony. Keeping secrets with God is like the keel on the bottom of the sailboat that keeps it from tipping over; *Father* wants you to have a deeper relationship with Him than anyone else knows.

The tendency is to ask *Father* to speak only when you are in trouble. People run to His voice when they face a crisis or a major decision, or when they want a quick fix. While *Father* welcomes such an approach, this is unhealthy. When you are *Abba's* child, it is far better to cultivate a consistent love relationship with *Father*, learning to hear His voice telling you that you are His favorite and learn to consistently receive His blessing. When you learn to hear His voice day-to-day, when crisis comes, He will speak clearly.

Learning to hear *Father's* voice is an essential part of re-parenting. We could say re-parenting starts with hearing and obeying. As you pray this prayer, be sure to listen for His voice and be prepared to do what He says:

Father, re-parent me in Jesus' name.

11

Father's Blessing

*F*ATHER IS ONE BIG blessing waiting to happen. The sooner you realize that, the better you'll be. You don't need to take a course or pass an exam to qualify; all you need to do is show up. *Father*'s blessing reminds me of another father's blessing.

During grad school, a friend and I both became first-time dads. We swapped war stories of late-night feedings, hypersensitive wives and dirty diapers. He told me about his cool habit: every night he would walk into his son's room at bedtime, put his hand on his boy's forehead, look him straight in the eye, and speak a blessing: "You are my son. I love you. I am so proud of you. You are a great blessing to me and your mom. I know God has big things for you. I am always here for you. I bless you, son." Some nights the blessing was shorter, and some longer, but every night he kept this habit.

Toward the end of the semester, however, my friend felt the time-crunch of too many pages to read, papers to write, and cups of coffee to drink. One night as he felt the stress of studies, he went into his fifteen-month-old son's nursery, pulled the covers up under the boy's chin and turned to leave without saying a word. It was then that he felt something that changed his life.

His son had wrapped his tiny finger around his pinky and hung on for dear life. The boy could only say a few words, barely waddle, but he had reached out his fat, little fist, grabbed his dad's finger, and pulled it towards his forehead.

My friend couldn't believe what was happening. It was a holy moment. The boy didn't need to say a word, but his vivid smile and bright eyes said it all—my friend knew immediately what his son was saying: "Daddy, I want your blessing. Don't leave my room without putting your hand on my head and saying those words to me. I love it when you do that. I need it, Daddy—I need it more than you may realize."

That night changed my friend's life. He had no idea that his son paid any attention to what he was doing, but this night told him everything. From that moment on, regardless of how late he needed to stay up, and how many cups of coffee he needed to drink, he never missed the opportunity to bless his son.

> ## The longing for dad's blessing is a picture of the inward longing for Dad's blessing.

The picture of that little boy pulling his dad's hand down to his own forehead is a picture of every girl and boy who longs for their father's blessing. This longing for dad's blessing is a picture of the inward longing for *Dad*'s blessing.

Thomas Merton helps us understand the unconditional nature of *Father*'s blessing:

One of the keys to real religious experience is the shattering realization that no matter how hateful we are to ourselves, we are not hateful to God. This realization helps us to understand the difference between our love and His. Our love is a need, His is a gift.[1]

I share this story with you because there is inside you, inside me, and inside everyone else, a longing for the *Father's* blessing. Whether your father put his hand on your forehead and spoke a blessing to you or not, you have a *Father* who puts His hand on your forehead and speaks a blessing. This story reminds me of the tear in Madonna's song "Papa Don't Preach" when she pleadingly asks her dad to not stop loving her.[2]

Threefold Blessing

Inside your chest are three invisible tanks that constantly need to be filled—the tank of acceptance, affection, and affirmation. Your acceptance tank needs to know you are okay, that you are accepted for who you are, and that you belong. Your affection tank needs to know that you are loved unconditionally, that you are appreciated, cared for—that you are special. Your affirmation tank needs to know that you fulfil a strategic role and that you are doing well. These three tanks are each filled by the *Father's* threefold blessing.

It is no coincidence that at the beginning of Jesus' ministry when *Father* spoke to His Son, He explicitly spoke this same threefold blessing over Jesus at His baptism. This blessing contains the threefold blessing that He has for you now: "You are my Son, whom I love; with you I am well pleased" (Luke 3:22). Notice that the threefold blessing from *Father* corresponds with the three needs inside your soul:

Acceptance—This is my Son

Affection—Whom I love

Affirmation—With you I am well pleased

The threefold blessing of *Father* corresponds to a three-fold groan within us. We sometimes think that in the pit of our stomach we long for a better job or bigger salary, but what we really long for is *Father's* blessing. The reason you have this threefold groan is because *Father* put it there—He built it into the pit of your stomach so that He would be the one to satisfy it. You can strive all you want to fill your three tanks, but you will remain empty until you receive the blessing from *Father*.

Acceptance

As *Abba's* child, you are fully accepted because you are in *Abba's* Son. You didn't earn *Father's* acceptance, and you can't forfeit His acceptance. Once you are in the Son, you are accepted as the Son, and you will never be rejected. For this reason, Merton encourages you:

> Surrender your poverty and acknowledge your nothingness to the Lord. Whether you understand it or not, God loves you, is present in you, lives in you, dwells in you, calls you, saves you, and offers you an understanding and compassion which are like nothing you have ever found.[3]

Affection

Now that you are *Abba's* child, you are loved unconditionally. Because you are in Christ, you are loved as Christ and nothing can separate you from *Father's* love. *Father's* love for you gives you power to conquer every fear you have—to kick out every worry, anxiety, terror, and fear. In order to cast out fear, you need the presence of a power that is greater than fear itself. *Father's* love is the power that can body-slam fear right out the door. The Bible, *Father's* Book, promises you, "There is no fear in love, but perfect love casts out fear" (1 John 4:18). Obviously perfect love does not refer to your love for Him, which will never be perfect, but to His love for you.

Affirmation

The words, "With you I am well pleased," are words God says to you frequently. These are the words you live to hear. Because you are now in Christ, you are gifted in Christ, called in Christ, and anointed in Christ. You are significant.

An essential motivation in your life as *Abba's* child is to feel the pleasure of God and to learn to hear His *attaboys* (or *attagirls*) throughout the day. King David learned to live as *Abba's* child and feel His pleasure through the day: "May the words of my mouth and the meditation of my heart be pleasing in your sight, O LORD, my Rock and my Redeemer" (Ps. 19:14, NIV). The apostle Paul exhorted *Father*-followers, "Try to discern what is pleasing to the Lord" (Eph. 5:10). Learning to feel *Father's* pleasure is the key to living under *Father's* blessing.

The healthier your soul becomes, the more you will desire every blessing you can get. One of the coolest qualities of *Father's* blessings is the fact that His blessings are unlimited. No matter how rich your dad was, most likely there were things he could not afford to give you; not so with your *Father*. When an orphan sits down at a dinner table, he knows there is only so much food to go around; not so with *Father*. The poverty mindset of the orphan spirit disappears

as you are re-parented. Jesus said frequently, "Freely you
have received, freely give" (Matt. 10:8, NKJV), and the more
thoroughly you are re-parented, the more blessing you will
receive and the more generous you will become.

Family Blessing

Father is not only one big blessing waiting to happen, His
blessing spills over into your nuclear family. When *Father*
initially called Abraham, He promised him a megaton family
blessing that would shake every other family on earth:

> I will make of you a great nation, and I will bless you and
> make your name great, so that you will be a blessing. I will
> bless those who bless you, and him who dishonors you I
> will curse, and in you all the families of the earth shall be
> blessed. (Gen. 12: 2–3)

This family blessing was a righteous carrot dangled in
front of Abraham his entire life. This same righteous carrot is
a potent picture of an all-important *Father* principle: *Father*'s
blessing on your human family is intended to be a healthy
motivation for you. The healthier you are, the hungrier you
will become for *Father*'s blessing on your nuclear family. There
is nothing inappropriate about wanting every blessing you can
get for yourself and for your family. The same carrot *Father*
held out to Abraham, He holds out to you today. He is sounding the dinner bell, and He wants you to "Come and get it!"

The Psalmist took the bait. He grabbed the carrot of
family blessing with both hands and prayed:

> May God be gracious to us and bless us
>   and make his face to shine upon us,   *Selah*
> that your way may be known on earth,
>   your saving power among all nations.

Let the peoples praise you, O God;
    let all the peoples praise you!
Let the nations be glad and sing for joy,
    for you judge the peoples with equity
    and guide the nations upon earth.   *Selah*
Let the peoples praise you, O God;
    let all the peoples praise you!
The earth has yielded its increase;
    God, our God, shall bless us.
God shall bless us;
    let all the ends of the earth fear him!

(Ps. 67)

It is wonderful for a father to put his hand on his child's forehead, look them straight in the eye, and speak a blessing, but *Father* does one better. Rather than simply touching the outside of your head, He floods your heart with His blessing. The apostle Paul knew what it was to receive the overflowing blessing of Christ: "I know that when I come to you I will come in the fullness of the blessing of Christ" (Rom. 15:29). Christ has a fullness of blessing because He comes from the fullness of *Father*. When you are in Christ, you too share the fullness of blessing, and you live out of the overflow.

As *Father* fills your three tanks every day—your acceptance, affection, affirmation tanks—re-parenting becomes natural. Now that you have received the fullness of the blessing of Christ, this six-word prayer will flow from your heart like never before:

Father, re-parent me in Jesus' name.

12

Father's Healing

*F*ATHER'S HOUSE IS A healing house. When you and I show up with our wounds, we don't need to wait three weeks for an appointment; we are not handed paperwork to fill out; we don't need to file insurance. We get to walk right in and see the Doctor.

Father doesn't dabble in healing in His spare time; He specializes in healing. I don't have a theology of healing; I just know He heals. Richard Foster put his finger on something profound:

> Today the heart of God is an open wound of love. He aches over our distance and preoccupation. He mourns that we do not draw near to him. He grieves that we have forgotten him. He weeps over obsession with muchness and manyness. He longs for our presence.[1]

Father heals on every level of life. Since people are trinitarian—spirit, soul, and body—*Father* heals on all three levels. When you were re-born, He not only healed your spirit, He raised it from the dead! *Father* also heals your body of physical illnesses and diseases. In my church in Atlanta, we see physical healings virtually every week, sometimes every day. I have seen five hundred people healed of every type of imaginable illness in one meeting. While I could literally fill a thick book of physical healing stories, our purpose now is to focus on soul care and soul healing.

The soul is your mind, will, and emotions, and *Father* wants you to know He heals each area and His healing is both immediate and progressive. As we have seen, His healing starts by healing your love receptors, and His healing flows from the inside out.

> ## We all get wounded and we all need healing; Jesus is the wounded Healer.

You and I live in a playground full of bullies—some of us have been bullies, and all of us have been bullied. Families, neighborhoods, workplaces, churches, mosques and synagogues all have their bullies, and we all have our wounds. Jesus made it clear that He came not for the healthy, but for those who are sick: "Those who are well have no need of a physician, but those who are sick. I came not to call the righteous, but sinners" (Mark 2:17).

In his song "The Boxer," Paul Simon sang about a fighter who carries the scars of every opponent who knocked him to the mat.[2] You and I are members of the walking wounded; we all get wounded and we all need healing. The good news is this: Jesus is the wounded Healer and every wound in you is connected to a wound in Him.

Pour Out Your Sorrows

Father is a healer. He doesn't need to rent a billboard or launch an ad-campaign to promote His healing. He doesn't need a flashing neon light to attract business. *Father* simply calls us into His oceanic, loving presence, and before we realize what is happening, we find ourselves becoming healthier. As we have seen, the essence of Christ's healing in our lives is the healing of our love receptors. Once our love receptors are healed, the emotional and physical healing flows.

Jesus actually bled from seven parts of His body—His sweat glands, His head, face, back, hands, feet, and side. Every wound in us is connected to a wound in Him and every wound in Him is healed. This means that our healing is found in Christ. I wrote *The Seven Wounds of Christ*, which focuses more specifically on this topic.[3]

Most healing we receive from *Father*, we receive simply by spending extended time in His presence. As we linger with *Father*, soaking in His healing presence, we receive deep, permanent healing without even being aware of it. Just as our immunity system wards off diseases and protects us from all kinds of illness of which we are completely unaware, so *Father's* love heals us from past wounds even when we are unconscious of them.

Father's house is a healing house, but in order for you to receive your healing, you need to be honest—no masks to wear, no labels to hide behind, no phoniness, and no hypocrisy. You can certainly be yourself in *Father's* house—raw, wounded, flawed, broken. You want to be honest, transparent, vulnerable.

In order for the healing of Jesus to flow into your wounds, He needs to access the point of pain. Like removing a bandage covering a wound, Jesus wants access, and you give Him access by telling Him what happened. It is necessary for you to re-visit the wound, go back in your memory, and think through the painful experience once again; but this time, do it with *Father*. Tell Him all about what happened. Then, ask *Father*, "Where was Jesus when I was being hurt?" I can almost guarantee you, *Father* will show you.

Infection

Wounds get infected. The hardest wounds to heal are those that become demon-infected. A wound becomes demon-infected when the devil speaks lies into your pain. The devils lies sound like thoughts that go through your mind, thoughts like these:

> *If God loved you this would never have happened.*
>
> *God was absent when you were being hurt.*
>
> *You were all alone when you were abused.*
>
> *You are a worthless piece of trash.*
>
> *You deserved better.*
>
> *God may love some people, but He obviously does not love you.*

Your infected wound often hides behind unforgiveness. Sometimes it's not just difficult to forgive; sometimes it's humanly impossible. When someone treats you with disrespect and dehumanizes you, it challenges your sense of justice. While you may not retaliate, letting go of bitterness and anger is hard. There is one factor, however, that completely changes the equation: Jesus. He was the most victimized person in history, and yet He unconditionally declared forgiveness from the cross: "*Father*, forgive them, for they know not what they do" (Luke 23:34).

It is important to understand that forgiveness does not minimize the offense, nor excuse it. It does not deny the hurt, nor diminish the severity. Forgiveness is simply giving up your right to get even. Forgiveness says, I will not hurt you even though you hurt me. Forgiveness is not an emotional response; it is a choice; a decision. Forgiveness is the fastest way to become Christ-like.

The most difficult step toward forgiveness is humbling yourself because unforgiveness sits on the ground of pride. Forgiveness is rooted in an "I-deserve-better" attitude. Unforgiveness is also a weapon that makes us feel stronger, a little bit safer, and this weapon is difficult to put down. It is difficult to relinquish resentment and retaliation until you see *Father* and His Son. If your wound is bigger than *Father*, you will never let go of unforgiveness; when you see that *Father* is bigger than your wound, you will be ready to let go of the weapon.

Father's love may sound wimpy, milquetoast, impotent, or anemic—but it is not. Don't be fooled! *Father's* love is the greatest force on earth. Listen to this description:

> Love is patient and kind; love does not envy or boast; it is not arrogant or rude. It does not insist on its own way; it is not irritable or resentful; it does not rejoice at wrongdoing, but rejoices with the truth. Love bears all things, believes all things, hopes all things, endures all things. (1 Cor. 13:4–7)

Antidote

Several years ago, I had a dream that taught me that love is the antidote to all the witchcraft in our world. The night before I was scheduled to fly to Congo, West Africa, I saw a picture in my dream of an enormous bank vault door that was two feet thick. Protruding from each edge of the vault door were three-inch steel bars that were extended into the door frame that locked it in place.

When I awoke, I was troubled by what I had seen. *Father* then said to my spirit, "This bank vault is a picture of the lockdown of witchcraft over the church in Congo." (I must admit, this revelatory dream gave me uncertainty about the effectiveness of my upcoming trip!)

When I fell back to sleep, I had a second dream in which I saw *Father's* love washing over the thick bank vault door. As His love flowed, I could hear the loud thud of each of the dead bolts being retracted one at a time, until the enormous bank vault door opened wide. I could then see a bright light shining from the other side. When I woke up, *Father* said to my spirit, "My love is the antidote for witchcraft. Lead My people in Congo to receive My love and I will open the door to My presence." These two dreams had a powerful impact on my time in Congo, and they have had a significant impact on my life.

When I told my two dreams to the church in Congo, something remarkable took place. An elderly Congolese gentleman came to the microphone and said with tears is his eyes, "Ten years ago I had exactly the same two dreams. What this man is telling you is true—this is a revelation from God. I have waited for the appointed time to tell anyone, but now is the appointed time." Before I could say a word, the entire group dropped to their knees in prayer and repentance. God activated their love receptors, and the healing love of *Father* swept through the room. God gave a breakthrough that day—He broke the curse of witchcraft and began to lovingly revive the Congolese church.

Witchcraft is manipulation or intimidation for the sake of domination and control. It tries to manipulate the strong and intimidate the weak in an effort to dominate. This spirit of control is all too present wherever people gather—in families, community groups, schools, businesses, churches, and governments.

Since this moment in Congo, I have led hundreds of thousands of people to break off the controlling, deadening spirit of witchcraft. Virtually every time people tell me, "When you were speaking to us, the Enemy was telling me not to trust you. I have been under the power of witchcraft my whole life, but today *Father's* love has overcome."

Several years ago, I spoke at a Christian school with several hundred students. Toward the end of my talk I called the students to respond to *Father's* love, and close to a hundred students stood to their feet, walked to the front of the auditorium and knelt down before *Father*.

One girl came and sat next to me. She said, "When you were talking a voice kept telling me, 'Stand up, walk out of the room, and go kill yourself.'" I was shocked, though glad she was so honest. "The voice told me," she added, "Whatever you do—do not go up and talk to that man."

I admired her honesty and her tenacity. She explained, "I knew the voice was lying to me when it told me to kill myself, so I figured it was lying when it told me not to talk to you. This is why I am talking to you."

We both chuckled. I then asked her a key question: "Have you ever heard that voice before?"

She had. She told me that ever since she was six years old that voice told her she was ugly, that she would never get married, and never have children. She told me she wanted to be set free, so I and a woman counselor led that girl to break off those lying voices and to receive *Father's* love. *Father* set her free that day and she was healed. Twenty years later, I met her parents in Canada, and they told me she was now married and the mother of three precious children. Hell lost another one! *Father's* love is the antidote for witchcraft.

It is important to understand these principles:

The wounded, wound; and the healed, heal.
The cursed, curse; and the blessed, bless.
The mocked, mock; and the honored, honor.
The hated, hate; and the loved, love.

Like draining puss from an ulcerated wound, Jesus will drain your toxic unforgiveness once you humble yourself and renounce your bitterness and resentment. Nothing becomes demon-infested faster than bitterness and unforgiveness. Unforgiveness attracts demons the way garbage attracts flies. Healing and forgiveness flow side by side, and Jesus is the source of both.

Healing at times seems to be instantaneous, and as we have said, at other times it is certainly a process. There are times we need friends, confidants, and therapists to help us, and at other times, *Father* does it all by Himself. In either case, whether it feels like it or not, His healing is a continual process. This prayer is an essential part of the process:

Father re-parent me in Jesus' name.

13

Father's Identity

WHEN YOU FIND *Father*, you get two for one—you find Him and you find yourself.

Perhaps the most gnawing question that growls in the hollow of your soul is, Who am I?

Our default answer tends to grab superficial labels. We have ethnic labels—I am Black, White, Latino, Asian; we have religious labels—I am Muslim, Christian, Jew, Atheist; we have issue labels—I am an addict, codependent, ADD, OCD; we have sexual orientation labels—I am straight, LGBTQ; we have music preference labels—I am pop, rap, heavy metal, jazz, country; we have career labels—I am an author, surgeon, salesperson, professor, lawyer, techy. At best our labels only tell part of the story.

When our daughter Andrea was three, she loved stickers—hearts, smiley faces, Mickey and Minnie. You could say, she never met a sticker she didn't like. It never seemed to matter what image was on the sticker; they were all fascinating to her as she played her imaginary games with her imaginary friends. One day Sherry took her to the local bookstore, owned and operated by a dear friend. Price tag stickers were everywhere, and Andrea thought she had entered sticker-heaven. When Sherry and the store owner were deep in conversation, Andrea was having the time of her life, pulling off the tags that had been meticulously placed on the appropriate book, CD or other store item and putting them all over her cute little legs.

When Sherry finally noticed our daughter, she was horrified. All the store owner could do was smile—you can't get too upset at a darling, though mischievous, three-year-old. We have often laughed at this incident, and it reminds us that our daughter is of greater value than all those stickers and store items. Her heart has no price tag and neither does her soul. Labels are fine for tomatoes, apples, and avocados, but they don't belong on you and me. God does not use labels—He does not use them, nor does He allow them.

> **LABELS ARE SUPERFICIAL, RESTRICTIVE.
> AT BEST, THEY DEFINE ONLY A SMALL
> PERCENTAGE OF YOUR TRUE SELF.**

As we said in the opening chapter, low self-esteem is the curse of our species. *Father* is the cure. Bob Dylan expressed our self-deception so well in the song entitled, "Abandoned Love."[1] He sings about being deceived "by the clown inside." Dylan's lyrics are so raw, so honest, and describe his vanity as nothing short of ball-and-chain bondage. Dylan has once again taken us to school. When we deceive ourselves and allow a label to define us, at the heart of our deception is vanity and pride, and the result is a ball and chain. At the end of the ball and chain is the fact that we have abandoned love.

Labels are superficial. While they may be accurate, they are incomplete. Labels are small and restrictive. At best, they define only a small percentage of your true self. What good is that? The lyrics of Bob Dylan's song, "Ain't No Man Righteous, No Not One" still gives me chills. When he points out that patriotism, flag waving, and nationalism can never be a substitute for an authentic relationship with God, it strikes a deep chord in me.[2] Your identity is more than skin deep. If you define yourself primarily by your ethnicity or your culture, you will likely miss your heart. If you define yourself by your issues, you will never know your true self. If you define yourself by your sexual orientation, you are settling for too little and you will always be self-deceived.If you define yourself by your music preference or your career path, you will never actually discover your true identity. Who you are is so much bigger than what you do.

Hypocrisy

When we speak of identity theft, we normally think of a stolen credit card, social security number, or bank account. Your worth cannot be defined, however, by your financial portfolio. The type of identity theft we are talking about now is far more costly—it can cost you your life.

What *Father* authentically does inside your heart, hypocrisy tries to synthetically fabricate. The transformation *Father* does inside you, hypocrisy tries to pin on your chest, like a plastic merit badge you buy at the dollar store. Jesus takes this matter of identity theft seriously. The call of *Father* is the call of honor. Concerning religious phonies of His day, Jesus said, "This people honors me with their lips, but their heart is far from me; in vain do they worship me, teaching as doctrines the commandments of men'" (Matt. 15:8–9). He warned His followers, "Beware of the leaven of the Pharisees, which is hypocrisy" (Luke 12:1).

Toward the end of his ministry on earth, Jesus issued a seven-fold woe-warning against this same insidious disease of phoniness and insincerity.

1. Hypocrisy is self-deceived. You preach but you can't practice: "You shut the kingdom of heaven in people's faces" (Matt. 23:13).

2. Hypocrisy is self-deceiving. You talk about heaven yet you live like hell: "For you neither enter yourselves nor allow those who would enter to go in" (23:14).

3. Hypocrisy is self-exalting. You work in *Father's* house yet avoid *Father*: "Woe to you, blind guides" (23:16–22).

4. Hypocrisy is self-destructive. You watch your diet, but binge on junk food: "You blind guides, straining out a gnat and swallowing a camel" (23:23–24).

5. Hypocrisy is self-justified. You clean your face, but your hearts are filthy: "You clean the outside of the cup and the plate, but inside they are full of greed and self-indulgence" (23:25–26).

6. Hypocrisy is people-pleasing and *Father*-insulting. You take your dress-shirts to the dry cleaners, yet your underwear stinks like dirty diapers: "You are like whitewashed tombs, which outwardly appear beautiful, but within are full of dead people's bones and all uncleanness" (23:27–28).

7. Hypocrisy is filled with hatred, judgementalism, and self-condemnation. You pompously honor the martyrs of the past, yet your parents murdered them: "You witness against yourselves that you are sons of those who murdered the prophets" (23:29–31).

No one intentionally sets out to be a hypocrite. When you ask a child what they want to be when they grow up, they will never say, "I want to grow up to be a hypocrite." Hypocrisy is never a goal; it just happens.

Idols

The pursuit of a false father is what is known as idolatry. Believe it or not, labels are linked to idols; and an idol is a projection of ourselves—our attempt to re-create God in our likeness. Ultimately, such an effort will not only fall short, but the label or idol will invariably be smaller than we are. For this reason, *Father* is zealous and jealous to protect you from such self-deception. You will discover, sooner or later, that *Father* is an expert idol-crusher.

When He said, "You shall not make for yourselves a carved image, or any likeness of anything that is in heaven above, or that is in the earth beneath" (Exod. 20:4), He followed it with the words, "For the LORD your God is a jealous God . . . showing steadfast love to thousands of those who love me" (20:5–6). The big deal with idols is not the external trinkets enshrined on our dashboards, but the internal trinkets we fondle. *Father* is a jealous lover because He alone can validate your life. "He yearns jealously over the spirit that he has made to dwell in us" (James 4:5); this means that *Father* yearns jealously over your spirit—over your heart. *Father* wants your heart and that is the issue. The reason *Father* declared war on idolatry is the same reason He declared war on hypocrisy. Idolatry is to *Father* what hypocrisy is to you. They are both false images, small, depersonalized and depersonalizing. Idolatry paints a false image of *Father*, and hypocrisy paints a false picture of you. They are both vicious enemies of re-parenting.

If *Father*'s jealousy confuses you, let me try to help. Jealousy is the desire to be first; more specifically, to be first in someone's heart and affections. While jealousy is a common feeling in all of us, it leads to problems because you and I are never intended to ultimately fill that spot in a human heart. *Father*, on the other hand, has every right to want to be first in hearts and affections, because He designed us this way. For this reason, while jealousy is destructive in the human heart, it is fully appropriate in *Father*'s heart.

True Self

Not until you discover that you are loved, and loved deeply, are you free to be yourself. Until you can be yourself, it's hard to find yourself. Brennan Manning admits,

> My greatest difficulty these past years has been bringing the imposter into the presence of Jesus. I am still inclined to flagellate the false self, to beat him mercilessly for self-centeredness, to get disheartened, discouraged, and decide that my alleged spiritual life is merely self-deception and fantasy.[3]

Henri Nouwen helps us cut through the claptrap of our self-deception:

> Over the years, I have come to realize that the greatest trap in our life is not success, popularity, or power, but self-rejection. Success, popularity, and power can indeed present a great temptation, but their seductive qualities often come from the way they are part of the much larger temptation of self-rejection.[4]

Remember, E.E. Cummings, a *Father*-seeker in his own rite, said it so well, "To be nobody-but-yourself—in a world which is doing its best, night and day, to make you everybody else—means to fight the hardest battle which any human being can fight; and never stop fighting."[5]

The battle for your identity is a battle for *Father*, and it is a battle worth fighting. It is a battle against superficiality, mediocrity, sterile religion, against the white noise of everyday life. It's a battle for home. You don't need to fight this battle yourself; *Father* created you to be nobody but yourself, and He is fighting for you. In fact, the best thing you have going for yourself in this quest is *Father*. He wants you to know that He fights for you because you are worth it. Realizing that He thinks the battle for you is worth fighting should certainly encourage your quest.

Brennan Manning knows by experience how challenging the quest for *Father* can be. One of his mentors, Larry Hein, says with a wink of irony,

> May all your expectations be frustrated, may all your plans be thwarted, may all your desires be withered into nothingness, that you may experience the powerlessness and poverty of a child and sing and dance in the love of God who is Father, Son, and Spirit."[6]

That sentence may be worth re-reading. When Thomas Merton was asked the question, "Who am I?" he responded, "I am loved by Christ."[7] Manning says it this way: "If I find Christ then I will find myself, and if I find my true self, I will find him."[8]

As we said, you will discover that *Father* is an expert idol-crusher. He removes the idols that mask the insecurities that cause you to hide, pose, and pretend. He removes your labels—labels like hopeless, lost, irreverent, worthless, trash. All your labels, stickers, or tattoos try to define you, but the result of all of them is the same—they devalue you. *Father* devalues no one. *Father* sees past your labels: "The LORD sees not as man sees: man looks on the outward appearance, but the LORD looks on the heart" (1 Sam. 16:7).

Dead Self

Father gives the best identity-finding advice: "If anyone would come after me, let him deny himself and take up his cross and follow me" (Matt. 16:24). Though it sounds counter-intuitive, your search for your true self often gets lost in the weeds. The genius behind this advice is that when you deny yourself and take up your cross, you are whacking away the deceptive weeds of your own arrogance and twisted ego. He goes on to explain our struggle for self-worth: "For what will it profit a man if he gains the whole world and forfeits his soul? Or what shall a man give in return for his soul?" (16:26). As we have said, self-worth will never be found in something beneath you, but only in something bigger. Because your worth is more than skin deep, it should never be defined by your culture, your issues, your music, sexual orientation, or career.

Just as Jesus was required to die and be buried in order to experience resurrection life, so are you and I. Even the apostle Paul knew that his twisted pride and false self had to be crucified: "I have been crucified with Christ. It is no longer I who live, but Christ who lives in me" (Gal. 2:20). He not only died with Christ and was raised with Christ, he exhorted all *Father*-followers to do the same: "You also must consider yourselves dead to sin and alive to God in Christ Jesus" (Rom. 6:11). Paul died to the excess baggage of his religious and ethnic issues, and to his sin addictions.

Breaking off your false self requires a death of sorts. *Father* calls you to die to your labels, to renounce your idols, and find your true identity in His Son. My self-death came prior to my thirtieth birthday. I decided to spend four days in a remote retreat center in central Florida with nothing but God, my Bible, and a single audio talk by Stephen Olford, a Christian leader in New York City.

> ## ALL GOD EVER EXPECTS FROM ANY OF US IS UTTER FAILURE.

I will never forget the moment. I was lying on my cot listening to Olford with my hands folded behind my neck looking up at the ceiling. At a critical moment in the talk, Olford said something I had never before heard: "All God ever expects from Stephen Olford is utter failure." I couldn't believe my ears. I hit rewind and played it again, and then a third time. It hit me like a sledgehammer and broke something inside me—it broke performance, striving, compulsion (even addiction). He went on to quote the words of Paul: "For I know that nothing good dwells in me, that is, in my flesh" (Rom. 7:18).

I fell to my knees on the wooden floor in my cabin like a crushed piece of chalk. My pulverized ego was speechless. The truth set me free. I began saying to *Father*, "All you ever expect from Fred Hartley is utter failure." I repeated it over and over again until it started to sink in.

That day I chose the cross. I chose to die to self. It was as if I was no longer kneeling on the floor; it was like lying on the cross and *Father* was driving nails into my wrists and ankles. I was being crucified with Jesus. My false identity, posing, hypocrisy, pretense was being drained. I humbled myself and *Father* poured His life into me. From that moment on, I was able to say with Paul, I am crucified with Christ. It is no longer I who live, but Christ who lives in me. Even though I was dying, I began to smile, even chuckle. It felt good to be free.

I-Doll

Several years ago, *Father* showed me an idol that was hiding in my heart—you could call it an I-doll; I would never have consciously erected a shrine to my own ego, but it was nevertheless putting up quite a fuss inside my heart. I had just returned from a five-day work trip in California where I had spoken to large crowds of college students and autographed more books than ever before in my life.

On my flight back to Atlanta, I was smiling in my business-class seat, rehearsing all the juicy details from my week to tell Sherry. Before I could even open my mouth, she told me what a disaster her week had been. Before she headed to bed, she handed me a long to-do list of overdue household chores for the next day. As exhilarating as my weekend was, her weekend was exhausting. She had been stuck at home with four demanding kids, while I was being treated like a rock star.

The next day, as I read through my to-do list, I felt anger welling up inside me. As I sat on my riding mower, I grumbled and complained about Sherry. The little spoiled, rotten child inside me wanted Sherry to treat me like a big shot instead of like a yard man. I think under my breath I even called her some dirty names.

But I will never forget what happened next. *Father* said, "Why are you complaining about your wife? Who do you think she is? She's your wife—not part of your fan club.

You are her husband, so quit pouting like a baby." His next words just about knocked me off my mower: "Your identity is not found in your fan club. What people think of you is not what should juice you. Who you are to Me and who you are to Sherry should mean more to you than who you are to everyone else on earth put together." *Father* then reminded me of His words, "Husbands, love your wives, as Christ loved the church and gave himself up for her" (Eph. 5:25).

This became a defining moment not only in my marriage, but in my self-discovery. It went deeper than my role as husband—it went to the heart of what it means to be *Abba's* child. I explicitly remember stopping my mower, turning off the key, and sitting there reflecting on what just happened. I repented and told God, "I have been worshipping the idol of my own little ego. I have been lapping up the applause of people like a narcotic, and I have become addicted to the adrenaline-rush of speaking in front of large crowds. And what makes it stink even worse is that I was self-righteously doing it all in Jesus' name."

Father was showing me a problem deeper than my marriage—He showed me a flaw in my heart. He reminded me of His words, "If anyone would come after me, let him deny himself and take up his cross and follow me." For the first time in my life, I understood what it was to identify and evict an idol inside my heart—the I-doll of arrogance, pride and a twisted ego. My I-doll was a puny, little, immature baby living in my heart that craved applause and pouted like a toddler when it was denied. I repented. I had never met *Father* on my mower before, but I did that day. He didn't just mow my pride; He scalped it!

I don't mean to superimpose my experience on you, but *Father*'s word to me is *Father*'s word to you: "If anyone would come after me, let him deny himself and take up his cross and follow me." This is a universal word because identity is a universal need. Your puny, little, immature self is the imposter— strutting like a peacock and distracting you from discovering your true identity. This is the best definition I have ever heard of humility: the willingness to be known for who I am.

Identity Recovered

Once you die to your twisted self, you are free to see who you truly are: you are a new person. As Paul was able to say, "For me to live is Christ" (Phil. 1:21). *Father* says again, "Therefore, if anyone is in Christ, he is a new creation. The old has passed away; behold, the new has come" (2 Cor. 5:17). You are ready to discover your complete identity in Christ.

- You are crucified with Christ. "I have been crucified with Christ. It is no longer I who live, but Christ who lives in me. And the life I now live in the flesh I live by faith in the Son of God, who loved me and gave himself for me" (Gal. 2:20).

- You are buried with Christ. "We were buried therefore with him by baptism into death, in order that, just as Christ was raised from the dead by the glory of the *Father*, we too might walk in newness of life" (Rom. 6:4).

- You died with Christ. "Do you know that all of us who have been baptized into Christ Jesus were baptized into his death?" (6:3).

- You were raised with Christ. "And raised us up with him" (Eph. 2:6).

- You are seated with Christ. "And seated us with him in the heavenly places in Christ Jesus" (Eph. 2:6).

- You are hidden with Christ. "For you have died, and your life is hidden with Christ in God" (Col. 3:3).

- You now have the full measure of the blessing of Christ. "I know that when I come to you I will come in the fullness of the blessing of Christ" (Rom. 15:29).

It is helpful to affirm your identity in Christ. You may find it useful to use this declaration to tell *Father* what He tells you about yourself:

Loving Father, I am Your child, adopted into Your family by Your Son, the Lord Jesus Christ.

I am crucified with Christ, dead and buried with Christ.

I am raised with Christ and seated with Him in heavenly places.

Because I am in Christ, I am loved as Christ, I am accepted in Christ, protected in Christ, honored, blessed, and gifted in Christ. For me to live is Christ and to die is gain.

Because I am in Christ, I am able to come boldly before Your throne and have access to all the blessings of Christ.

I am under the authority of Christ, and I come in the authority of Christ, and in the full measure of the blessing of Christ.

Now that you have removed your labels, idols and false self, you are ready for re-parenting. Every day *Father* is prepared to validate your identity, fill you with His pleasure, and embolden you to live life with confidence, zeal and authority. This prayer will make more sense to you every day because re-parenting strengthens your identity:

Father, re-parent me in Jesus' name.

14

Father's Calling

YOUR IDENTITY AND your calling are inseparably linked—you don't get one without the other, although the two are not identical.

The two greatest questions you will ever answer in life are these: *Who am I?* and *Why am I here?* Identity is who you are; calling is why you are.

Both your identity and your life-calling are like your fingerprints and your DNA—they are one hundred percent unique to you. No one else on earth can take your place. You may have a biologically identical twin, but no one else has your identical calling.

The beauty of *Father* is that He reveals both. Both your identity and your calling are in Christ. Once He shows you *who* you are, He will show you *why.*

Your job is not your calling; neither is your career. You get paid to do a job, but your calling is priceless. Your job is beneath you; your calling is above you. You can get fired from your job, but not your calling. Your job can become an idol, but not your calling. Your job is given by people, while your calling is given by God. No matter how much you love your job, there are days it will wear you out; your calling, on the other hand, will always juice you. You share your employment with thousands of others in the workforce who do similar tasks; your calling is entirely unique to you. For this reason, you can go to school to learn a trade, or take a course to develop a skill, but only *Father* equips you for your calling.

It may be helpful to keep in your mind a clear distinction between your calling and your career. In my earlier book, *Hearts on Fire*, this list was included as a reminder:

Your Calling	Your Assignment
Above you	Beneath you
Who you are	What you do
Eternal	Temporary
Universal	Local
100% unique to you	Shared with others
Linked to your identity	Linked to your activity
Always refreshing	Sometimes exhausting
Always high	Often low

My wife is a world-class mother. She poured herself into our four children with deepest joy and affection. From infancy to adulthood, she enjoyed every moment of motherhood. When our youngest son Andrew went to college, for the first time in twenty-seven years, we were empty nesters, and the transition for her was hard. Her identity, calling, and personal fulfillment were so linked to her role as mom, she struggled not only with the emotional loss, but with her calling.

Then *Father* gave her a fuller revelation of her calling. He said, "Precious daughter, Sherry, you are correct in thinking I have called you to be a mother. But you have been thinking too small. Your four children were your assignment and you have done well. Your calling, however, is to mother many.

Don't limit yourself to simply mothering your four kids; I have called you to love, nurture, and mother many."

This was both a freeing and a healing moment for Sherry. She suddenly realized that an empty nest did not diminish her self-worth. *Father* has since brought many precious people into her life whom she serves as a godly mentor and mother.

> **WHEN YOU ARE ABBA'S CHILD,**
> **YOUR IDENTITY, LIFE-PURPOSE,**
> **CALLING, ARE ALL IN CHRIST.**

The quest for calling will drive you in one of two directions: toward *Father*, in whom you will most certainly find your calling, or toward self, in whom you will come up frustrated and unfulfilled. Augustine, one of my favorite *Father*-thinkers, made a profound observation: "There can only be two basic loves, the love of God unto the forgetfulness of self, or the love of self unto the forgetfulness and denial of God."[1]

If this sounds like a lofty, unattainable promise, it's not; it's *Father*. Welcome to the only realm in which you can thrive—welcome to the love of *Father*. The reason you find yourself when you find *Father* is because when you are *Abba's* child, your identity, life-purpose, calling, are all in Christ. As you read these words from *Father*-thinker Henri Nouwen, understand that Beloved refers to us, not Him:

> What is required is to become the Beloved in the commonplace of my daily existence and, bit by bit, to close the gap that exists between what I know myself to be and the countless specific realities of everyday life. Becoming the Beloved is pulling the trust revealed to me from above down into the ordinariness of what I am, in fact, thinking, talking about, and doing from hour to hour.[2]

Honor

Calling and honor are inseparable; when you discover your calling, you will discover honor. With honor comes dignity, significance, and fulfillment in life. It is essential to understand that calling and honor are never grabbed, only given. If you attempt to grab them independently, you will come up empty. You and I were never made for autonomous honor nor self-imposed calling.

Self-imposed calling and autonomous honor are the very definition of evil. The devil was the first one to make the fatal mistake of grabbing both, and he has been coming up empty ever since.

I am not saying that the discovery of your calling and your quest for honor is difficult—it's not difficult, it's impossible. Striving for self-esteem is a wearisome, never-ending, uphill climb. Henri Nouwen even admitted, "For a very long time, I considered low self-esteem to be some kind of virtue."[3] There was a time in my life I could identify with this distorted thought. Perhaps you can, too.

Father made discovering your calling and gaining dignity impossible without Him, because you and I were made to discover our identity and calling in *Father*. This is part of our human genome that reveals the genius of *Father*. This is why David, one of the greatest statesmen and military leaders in history, said to *Father*, "You . . . are . . . my glory, and the lifter of my head" (Ps. 3:3). Let me say it again: the source of human dignity is *Father*. David did not find his calling in governmental leadership or military prowess, but in *Father*.

You can't give what you don't have. An orphan-heart is incapable of showing honor because it has have never received honor. Nouwen gets even more vulnerable and raw:

Against my own best intentions, I find myself continually striving to acquire power. When I give advice, I want to be thanked; when I give money, I want it to be used my way; when I do something good, I want to be remembered. I might not get a statue, or even a memorial plaque, but I am constantly concerned that I not be forgotten, that somehow I will live on in the thoughts and deeds of others.[4]

Honor that we grab for ourselves is illusive and short-lived at best. You and I strive for honor the way we try to grab for a bar of soap—the moment we think we have it in our fist, it squirts across the shower floor. The only honor that sits on us for any extended time is honor that comes from somewhere outside of ourselves. Brennan Manning is right when he says, "My dignity as *Abba's* child is my most coherent sense of self."[5]

Mother Teresa knew *Father's* heart well and summarized her calling in life this way:

Love is giving. God loved the world so much that he gave His son. Jesus loved the world so much, loved you, loved me, that he gave his life and he wants us to love as he loved and so now we have also to give until it hurts. True love is a giving and giving until it hurts.[6]

In a sense, each of our life-callings, though expressed differently, are callings to love. No matter who you are, love is your highest calling, and love for *Father* is on top of your highest calling.

Gifting

No matter how smart and successful you are, *Father* wants you to know that you are gifted. In fact, your gifts make you not only valuable, but significant. You have a role to play, not only in time, but in eternity. Your unique gifting is inseparably linked to your calling. As *Father* says, "The gifts and calling of God are irrevocable" (Rom. 11:29). Discovering your unique gifts or supernatural empowerment is essential to discovering your calling. While this is not the place to dig extensively into the supernatural abilities *Father* has given you, it is helpful to know for certain that He considers you worthy of such gifts. *Father* has never yet made a bad investment—and you will surely not be the first!

Anointing

Anointing is one of my favorite words. It is a word picture of oil being poured on a person to set them apart to fulfill their *Father*-calling. Anointing is the supernatural empowerment He gives all His children to fulfill their calling. The beauty of anointing is that it is a win-win: ultimately anointing is a win for *Father* because it supernaturally makes Him look good, and it's a win for you because it supernaturally makes you do good.

Don't allow the word *anointing* to confuse you—it's not a lucky-winner lottery ticket, nor a door prize available to a select few. Anointing is for all *Abba*'s kids because anointing is in Christ. Better yet, anointing is Christ. The name Christ *literally means* anointed. Jesus is the anointed One, and the anointing One. Jesus is the One in whom you find your identity, your calling, your gifting, and your anointing. Hopefully you are beginning to see a pattern.

When Jesus announced His calling, He announced His anointing because calling and anointing are inseparable. Reading from the scroll of Isaiah the prophet, written seven hundred years prior, these words precisely described Jesus' calling:

The Spirit of the Lord is upon me,
    because he has anointed me
    to proclaim good news to the poor.
He has sent me to proclaim liberty to the captives
    and recovering of sight to the blind,
    to set at liberty those who are oppressed,
to proclaim the year of the Lord's favor.

Luke 4:18–19

Notice how the Son knew the successful completion of His calling was contingent on His anointing. This means that during the three years of His Palestinian ministry, Jesus lived His calling out of His Holy-Spirit-anointed humanity, which is exactly how you and I are to live our calling.

Just as Jesus claimed *Father's* anointing on Himself at the beginning of his ministry, He offers *Father's* anointing to the rest of us. At the end of His mission, He said, "Stay in the city until you are clothed with power from on high" (Luke 24:49). Being clothed with power was Jesus' way of telling us to receive Holy Spirit anointing and empowerment to fulfill our calling.

Some people are more successful than others at their profession, but it's nice to know that you are guaranteed success at fulfilling your God-given calling. *Father* promises, "He who calls you is faithful; he will surely do it" (1 Thess. 5:24). Regardless of how messed-up you may feel, no matter how many times you fail, or how long it takes you to get it right, when you are in Christ, you will succeed.

Fulfillment

The fulfillment of your calling means two things—the successful completion of tasks related to your calling, and the sense of genuine satisfaction you feel. Both are valid and both are needed. It's the second part of fulfillment—the inner sense of *attaboy!*—where we need help.

As important as it is for you to feel love, *Father* wants you to feel significant, and He wants you to feel it for two reasons: Your own significance is an accurate view of reality; and He made you with a capacity to feel His pleasure. He wants to activate your receptors on a daily basis to not only receive His love but to also feel His pleasure. Jesus obviously lived with a heightened sense of *Father's* pleasure. When He said, "I always do the things that are pleasing to him" (John 8:29), He affirmed that He always feels *Father's* pleasure. David also continually felt *Father's* pleasure, and even prayed, "May these words of my mouth and this meditation of my heart be pleasing in your sight, LORD, my Rock and my Redeemer" (Ps. 19:14, NIV). Paul continually felt *Father's* pleasure, and exhorted others: "Try to discern what is pleasing to the Lord" (Eph. 5:10). Feeling *Father's* pleasure is an essential part of re-parenting.

Since your calling, identity, gifting, and anointing are all in Christ, this means your fulfillment is also in Christ. Jesus fulfilled His calling out of His Spirit-anointed humanity, and so do you. As Christ continually felt *Father's* pleasure, He wants you to continually feel His pleasure as well. Feeling His pleasure and re-parenting go hand in hand. Re-parenting is the context in which calling is revealed. Every champion recorded in the Bible received their calling in a re-parenting encounter with *Father*. If you want to grow in your calling, in one way or another, this prayer is part of the process:

Father, re-parent me in Jesus' name.

15

Father's House

YOUR LONGING FOR belonging is a longing for *Father's* house. *Father* loves family, and aren't you glad He expanded His family to include you and me. One day He will gather us together for the ultimate family reunion, and it will be a blast!

Home is a place of belonging, acceptance, and unconditional love where you don't need to perform. Home is the place where you can be yourself—raw, vulnerable, exposed, without fear of rejection, mockery, rejection, or abandonment. Home is where *Father* is waiting to welcome you. For an orphan, home can be a tormenting illusion—an empty promise—*don't talk to me about a fantasy home if you cannot deliver*, an orphan thinks. *Don't talk to me about Father if He will not adopt me. Don't get my hopes up only to let me down.*

Home is a place for which an orphan longs, but of which they are not sure even exists. Before you can believe in a place called home, you must believe in a person called *Father*.

When you think about heaven, you may imagine a place that is boring, where we do nothing but float around on clouds and yawn, and where the highlight of every day is nap time—with chubby little angels wearing tutus and flying around like bumblebees. You may think of a place that constantly plays bad music, where you will feel awkward and out of place. There are probably more misconceptions about *Father's* house than there are about UFO's. Just as we tend to project our own image on God and distort Him in the process, we also tend to project our image on His house. If this is what you think, you are in for a pleasant surprise. When you are in *Father's* presence, you will be more alive, and more yourself, than ever.

Heaven

One evening when my mother and her doctors thought for sure she was dying, I sat on the edge of her bed and talked with her about *Father's* house. It was a night I will never forget. The more I talked, the more she came alive. The more insight I gave her about heaven, the faster her heart beat. Every few minutes, she would light up, interrupt me, and exclaim, "Really! Oh, Fred, tell me more! O my! Why hasn't anyone told me this before—tell me more; O Fred, I've been going to church for years, and I've never heard this—tell me more!"

As I talked with my mom about her eternal home, I was not in any way trying to impress her nor entertain her. My objective was not to be sensational or edgy—I was simply telling her things *Father's* book clearly says about *Father's* house. What began as a two-minute homily, quickly became a forty-five-minute pep rally, and what I told my mom on the edge of her mattress might be useful to you.

The most obvious reality about heaven is that when you arrive in *Father's* house, you will feel right at home—in fact, you will be more at home than you have ever been in your life. Rather than being dead, you will pleasantly be more yourself and more alive than ever, and there are reasons for this.

At the pearly gates, in case you didn't realize it, you will see a sign as you enter, so to speak, that says, check your masks and labels here. It's not that we will leave our culture, skin color and personalities at the gate—of course, we will still retain the uniquenesses of our own personhood—but we will leave our labels. Without the restraints and inhibitions, we will be even more unique and fearless. No more posing, no trying to impress anyone because there will not even be a tinge of rejection.

> **IN FATHER'S HOUSE, YOU WILL BE PERFECTLY LOVED, WITH NO FEAR, SHAME, OR GUILT.**

There will be no fear in *Father's* house because you are now and forever in the presence of greatness—no fear of failure, of being alone, of exposure or humiliation, of rejection, hurt, or disappointment. There will be no shame or guilt. You will now have the experience of being perfectly loved by *Father* and by everyone else in the family, and perfect love will cast out all fear. All the unfair comparisons of keeping up with the Kardashians will end when you enter *Father's* house.

Comparison is a curse of our culture, and social media has put comparison on steroids. Jealousy and envy are the active byproduct, and self-hatred and depression are the result. Comparison always puts a mute in our trumpet and causes us to drive with our foot on the brake. Whatever we enjoy is never as good as what others have. *Father's* house, on the other hand, removes all unrighteous comparison; it takes the mute out of the trumpet, it takes the foot off the brake, so you can enjoy every moment to the full.

Part of the explosive joy of heaven is the joy of discovery. There will be a sort of daily news feed in heaven, telling the latest discoveries. Moses, Abraham, Isaiah and John will be offering classes on the backstory to the Bible, and people will be utilizing their best gifts and talents. Scientists on earth will be scientists in heaven, only their laboratories will be far more sophisticated, and rather than competing with each other, they will be complimenting each other.

Pioneers and explorers on earth will be pioneering the vast domain of the galaxies, and many other galaxies. Financial investors on earth will be utilizing their skills and allocating funds, but rather than working with millions and billions, they will be working with trillions and quadrillions (1 followed by 15 0's). As *Father* says, "The gifts and the calling of God are irrevocable" (Rom. 11:29), and you will be a gazillion times more juiced and more productive as you exercise your gifts and calling in *Father's* house.

There is a common misconception about heaven that suggests the moment we arrive we will instantly know everything. This is based on a misunderstood Bible verse that says, "Now I know in part; then I shall know fully, even as I am fully known" (1 Cor. 13:12). But just stop and think about this: knowing in full does not mean your knowledge will happen instantly; rather it suggests that nothing will be hidden or beyond discovery. While God is all-knowing, you will never be all-knowing because you will never become God. Part of the joy of living is the joy of discovering, and heaven is full of discovery.

A child who enjoys a piggyback ride around the house on his dad's shoulders says as soon as the ride is over, "Again dad; let's do it again!" You and I in *Father's* house will say a hundred billion times, "Again, *Dad*; let's do it again!" He will take us on better-than-piggyback-rides over and over and over again. Heaven is where new music is always being written, new art is always being created, new land pioneered and developed, and new technology discovered. Colors never seen before will be on display every day in heaven. New tastes will be shared, and new galaxies discovered.

While this chapter on *Father*'s house easily deserves an eight-hundred-page volume, I just want to include one further reality which I find thoroughly captivating: *Father*'s house will be ever-expanding. We already know that *Father* is the consummate scientist, the epic artist and musician, the one-of-a-kind inventor, the stand-alone creator, and the King of Kings and Lord of Lords. There is absolutely no reason to suspect that He is done exercising the fullness of His creative skills. Why would we think that His best days are behind Him, or that our best days are behind us? This is foolishness.

The same *Father* who created Tyrannosaurus, Stego-saurus, Brachiosaurus and Ankylosaurus, which are already extinct, will certainly create new species of previously unseen turtles, birds, fish, mammals and amphibians. The same *Father* who has already created our solar system and thousands of others, will certainly continue creating a gazil-lion more that will make ours seem like a *Risk* boardgame or *Settlers of Catan*.

Isaiah the prophet was onto something when he said, "Of the increase of his government and of peace there will be no end" (Isa. 9:7). Increase requires expansion, growth, de-velopment, pioneering, leadership, problem-solving, and all the challenges we were made to conquer. Einstein, Hawking and Musk may have no explanation for an ever-expanding universe, but *Father* does. The explanation is simply *Father*.

Hell is just as real as heaven, and everything heaven is, hell is not. Hell is boring, ever-shrinking, same-old same-old. Hell is phoniness, masks and hypocrisy. Hell is wounds that never heal, songs that never end, a basketball that's always flat, a car that won't start, and a friend that you will never, ever see again.

Hell is real and hell is final. Hell is the sinking feeling in the pit of your stomach of regret, shame, loss and fail-ure. Hell is memories of hands you didn't shake, cards you didn't send, phone calls you never dialed, children you never hugged, and opportunities you completely missed.

Hopefully, by now you realize that all good boys and girls don't go to heaven; they go to hell. Good from our per-spective is relative, and *Father* doesn't grade on a curve. As good as you may be, your good is not good enough. *Father's* standard for good is His Son; if you have the Son, you have heaven; if you don't, you have hell.

There is a ranch in Florida with a huge sign that tow-ers over the main entrance which reads, "Almost Heaven." While I'm sure the owner's intentions were good, as impres-sive as it sounds, almost heaven is hell. Heaven is not horse-shoes—you don't get points for coming close. *Father* didn't send His Son because close was good enough; He sent His Son because no one can get to heaven on their own. To get to heaven, you need the goodness of the Son.

The final reality of heaven may be the most obvious: In *Father's* house, Jesus is the big deal. He is the life of the party, the center of attention. While we will not always be singing festive songs in His honor, all the work we do and the time we spend in *Father's* house will be to the praise and enjoyment of the Son. These words will be fulfilled:

> Therefore God has highly exalted him and bestowed on him the name that is above every name, so that at the name of Jesus every knee should bow, in heaven and on earth and under the earth, and every tongue confess that Jesus Christ is Lord, to the glory of God the *Father*. (Phil. 2:9–11)

While the name of Jesus will cause every knee to bow, and every tongue to confess that Jesus Christ is Lord, notice that all praise goes back to *Father*—"to the glory of God the *Father*." This is, after all, *Father's* house, and He ultimately gets the glory.

Feels Like Home

Home is where you belong. The four words, this feels like home, are defined differently for each one of us, but we all know what they mean. We each have our own unique metrics by which we determine what feels like home, but we intuitively know what home feels like when we get there. Though our standards may be subjective—more art than science—you and I and the almost 8 billion other people on the planet know what it feels like. We may not be able to draw a picture nor put it into words, but we each know what it is, and what it is not.

When Nike ran the "Bo-Knows" ad campaign, it struck a chord. Bo Jackson was once the most famous man in America. He was the first legitimate two-sport, all-star professional athlete and for the better part of ten years was the busiest, most high-profile businessman.

When Nike initiated the aggressive "Bo-Knows" campaign, they almost immediately doubled the sales of their cross-training shoe. Bo-Knows baseball, Bo-Knows football, Bo-Knows lacrosse, Bo-Knows everything, or so it seemed. He had more toys in his garage than he knew what to do with—a Viper, Mercedes, Harley Davidson, and more.

In 1989, he hit 32 home runs, drove in 105 runs for the Kansas City Royals, and was named the MVP of the All-Star Game. Ten days after the baseball season ended, he joined the LA Raiders, and in just eleven games, rushed 15,000 yards. The following year he was picked for the Pro Bowl.

But then, following a hip surgery, without so much as a news conference or any fanfare, he seemed to drop off the face of the earth.

And no one seemed to notice, either—that is no one but *Sports Illustrated*. They did a touching article in true *Sports Illustrated* brilliance entitled, "What Became of Bo?" It all came down to two words: his kids. He wanted to have more of a relationship with his kids than his dad had with him. He said, "Do you know what I thought a father was? A man that came to the house every month and a half and left $20 on the table."[1] Essentially Bo grew up fatherless.

> My father has never seen me play professional baseball or football. . . . I tried to have a relationship with him, gave him my number and said, "Dad, call me, I'll fly you in." Can you imagine? I'm Bo Jackson, one of the so-called premiere athletes in the country, and I'm sitting in the locker room and envying every one of my teammates whose dad would come in and talk, have a beer with them after the game. I never experienced that.[2]

One day, Bo's son Nick casually asked, "Why is Daddy never home? Does he have another home with more kids?" That innocent question hit Bo between the eyes like a fast ball—it was *déjà vu* all over again. He seemed to reflect to his own children the same kind of father he had when he was growing up. He saw himself reflecting his own dad's irresponsible patterns. In no time, Bo told his teams and sponsors that he was done with the exhausting treadmill and it was time to be a dad. "Whenever I had free time, I'd spend the whole day with my kids." Essentially, he gave up a $10-million-a-year job in order to watch his kids get off the school bus every afternoon and tuck them in every night. Good choice.

As Bo's lifestyle changed in relationship to his children, his heart changed towards his dad, too. "I decided to see my father after all," he says. He drove to Birmingham to see his dad after hip rehab. "We sat down, had a long talk, and I told him the things that had been eating at me. Things are looking up." Just two weeks prior to the *Sports Illustrated* article going to print, the phone in Bo's workroom rang. It was his dad. "'Sitting in this chair,' Bo says, 'Right here. First time he ever called. Took him thirty-two years to realize he had a son that loved him.'"[3]

> **I NEED A PLACE WHERE I AM LOVED, ACCEPTED, HONORED, AND RESPECTED, AND SO DO YOU.**

It is remarkable how often success in life, or the pursuit of it, distracts us from our true calling. It often takes a fast ball between the eyes to wake us up—even an innocent question from our children. What's worth more than $10 million? That's easy—home. Bo Jackson made the right choice when he chose family. He knew home was where he belonged.

I need a place where I am loved, accepted, honored, and respected, and so do you. You need a seat at the table and a role to fulfill in the family—a place where you would be missed, and a family that would not be complete without you. This is what you and I find in *Father's* house.

Full of Surprises

The *Father's* house will be full of surprises—in a sense, His house will be one big surprise party! Perhaps the three biggest surprises will be these: (1) who will be there; (2) who will not be there; and (3) that I will be in there.

The *Father's* house is a huge house, diverse in every way—African, Asian, Latino, European, American, Lithuanian, and Aboriginal. Every nationality, ethnicity, and religious background will be represented—Jew, Catholics, Muslim, Buddhist, Hindu, Sikh, agnostic, and atheist-background people. Every imaginable political party will be represented—Marxist, Anarchist, Republican, Democrat, Socialist, Globalist, Nationalist. Every philosophical background will be represented—humanist, materialist, hedonist, nihilist, socialist, capitalist, deist. Wealthy and poor, royalty and peasants. down-and-outers and up-and-outers will all be there because we will share a common blood-line and a common *Father*.

One of the biggest surprises of all in *Father's* house is that there will be no temples, mosques, synagogues, or churches. We will not go to church; we will be the church. We will not go to worship; we will be in a perpetual state of worship. It is not surprising that the Son said, "But the hour is coming, and is now here, when the true worshipers will worship the *Father* in spirit and truth, for the *Father* is seeking such people to worship him" (John 4:23–24).

You may think that continual worship in *Father's* house might become boring and repetitious, but you are in for yet another surprise. Music icon Kesha never knew the identity of her father yet wrote a song from the longings of her heart entitled, "Father-Daughter Dance." Wrestling with her pain, she sings a lament to the painful reality that from birth to death she will never enjoy a daddy/daughter dance.[4] The longing of her heart goes beyond a reunion with her biological dad; it reflects a far deeper longing that will be fulfilled in our *Father's* house. For every daughter and son in *Father's* house, there will be the *Father*-dance you always wanted.

Culture of Honor

The great characteristic in *Father's* house is the healing presence of honor and dignity—the honor you always wanted and the dignity you never got. Love and mutual respect will permeate the place. Whoever loves *Father* loves family. Healthy families are like waterfalls—they are both impressive and captivating. People travel for days and sit for hours at Victoria Falls, Niagara Falls, Yosemite Falls, and the tallest waterfall in the world—Angel Falls in Venezuela with 328 feet of uninterrupted falling water. But the tallest (interrupted) waterfall of all is in Hawaii. It cascades over 3,000 feet continually moving from one pool of water to another, until it reaches the bottom of this impressive mountain. Similarly, *Father's* love is a cascading waterfall, with Jesus in the middle. The Son said, "As the *Father* has loved me [waterfall #1], so have I loved you [waterfall #2]. Abide in my love."[5] And again he said, "This is my commandment, that you will love one another [waterfall #3] as I have loved you [waterfall #2]."[6] Clearly, this means that the success of your ability to love people—particularly people different than you—is based on two words: receive and release. Receive and release was the key to the Son's success. Jesus freely received the *Father's* love and freely released the *Father's* love. In turn, Jesus loved His disciples and taught them to receive and release. The problem most *Father*-followers have is the problem of retention. All you need to do to ruin a great waterfall is to retain water. The way to ruin a good family is to retain love.

One of the most exciting parts of visiting a great waterfall is feeling the force of the spray; nothing makes us feel more at home than feeling the force of love through family members. Jesus reinforced this receive-and-release principle when He taught His disciples, "Freely you have received; freely give" (Matt. 10:8, NIV).

Same Blood

A family is defined by people who share a common blood-line. This is true biologically, and it is true in *Father's* house. Jesus came to expand the family, to add seats at the table, and He successfully completed His mission by shedding his blood. He no longer wanted to be the only Son who could legitimately call God *Father*—He wanted to include you and me. He bled in order to donate His bloodline to people like us. *Father's* house is now full of adopted daughters and sons—former orphans—who now get an equal share of the inheritance. You and I are blood-brothers and blood-sisters through the blood-line of Jesus.

The most zealous we see Jesus was in defense of *Father's* house. It's the only time we see His forehead turn beet red in anger and the tendons in His neck get as tight as piano wire. He grabbed tables and turned them upside down. He grabbed cash registers and tossed them across the dance floor. He wove together strips of leather to make a horse whip and used it to drive people out the door. With an uncharacteristic forceful-ness, He demanded, "'My house shall be called a house of prayer,' but you make it a den of robbers" (Matt. 21:13).

A den of thieves, by the way, is not where thieves go to steal, but where they hide after they have stolen; a house of prayer, on the other hand, is where you meet with God. Jesus was, thereby, saying: "I came to make *Father's* house a place to meet God, but you have made it a place to hide from God." He put His finger on the central issue of *Father's* house—encountering Him. While religious rituals will al-ways create a safe place for us to hide, Jesus came to remove the masks, pull back the curtain, and lead us to a face-to-face encounter with *Father* in *Father's* house.

> ## As sisters and brothers, you and I share a common Father.

The most dominant feature of any family is that families share a common father. As sisters and brothers, you and I certainly share a common *Father*. The most thrilling and invigorating characteristic of *Father's* house will be His pres-ence. There will be no need of lamp fixtures in the *Father's* house because His Son will radiate and fill each room with His brilliance.

Join the Family

As *Abba's* child, you now have a new job—to invite oth-ers into the family. Charles Spurgeon was reduced to infancy when he encountered *Father's* love:

> O Blessed Spirit of God! Let us all now feel that we are the children of the great Father and let our child-like love be

warm today; so shall we be fit to go to and proclaim the Lord's love to the prodigals who are in the distant land among the pigs."[7]

You and I are part of the most important search and rescue team ever assembled. In the film *The Guardian*, Kevin Costner plays a world-class rescue diver in the treacherous waters off the northern coast of Alaska. His heroism is un-paralleled, risking life and limb to rescue people he never met. The heroism, sacrifice, and honor of risking your life to save another represents what Jesus did for us, and what we can do for others. Jesus affirms such sacrificial love of family: "Greater love has no one than this, that someone lay down his life for his friends" (John 15:13).

While you and I may never jump out of a helicopter into the frigid waters of the Arctic Ocean, you and I have the noble duty to love our next-door neighbors and serve them each day. Hell is real, and a far worse reality than drowning in the turbulent Arctic Ocean. Part of the honor of family is both the search and rescue of fellow orphans who are still lost and welcoming them into the family. The ultimate role you and I have as *Abba's* kid is to welcome other orphans to the family.

Father's house is where re-parenting is done best—we could call it re-parenting on steroids. The revolutionary six-word prayer we keep repeating is a prayer we will actually never stop praying; it will take us through time into eternity. Once we get inside *Father's* house, we will then enjoy the answer to this prayer with ever-increasing gusto:

Father, re-parent me in Jesus' name.

16

Father's Joy

FATHER LAUGHS. THE reason you have the capacity to enjoy a good laugh is because *Father* does. I am not talking about a mere smirk or snicker—I am talking about unrestrained belly-laughter, laughter that can be heard two blocks away. Healthy people laugh and you can be sure *Father* is healthy. This may shock you, but *Father* has a better sense of humor than you do.

Joy and laughter characterize *Father's* house. If your image of *Father* is stiff, pompous and austere, you may not know Him as well as you think. If you think for a moment that spending time with *Father* in His house will be boring, as we said, you will be pleasantly surprised. John Piper writes, "It is impossible, therefore, that God is boring. If we find him boring, we are like five-year-old's who find sex boring. The problem is not with sex, nor is the problem with God."[1]

It may surprise you to learn that the dominant characteristic in *Father's* house is joy. *Father* is a happy Guy—not like fat-cheeked Santa, who bellows his predictable ho-ho-ho and seems out of touch with reality. *Father* is happy because He lives in a higher reality and faces every challenge on earth with hope and confidence, knowing He is a redeemer, and in the end, He and His kids win—every wound is healed; every tear is wiped away; His enemies become His footstool; the bad guys lose and His kids get the inheritance. More than simply being happy, *Father* is full of joy. *Father*'s book shows Him laughing no fewer than six times.[2] We read, "He who sits in the heavens laughs [*sachaq*]" (Ps. 2:4). *Sachaq* is used thirty-six times in the Bible and it means to laugh with pleasure, dance, sport, play. Even King David danced [*sachaq*] before the Lord with all his might.[3]

In *Father*'s house, where there will be millions and billions of family members, it will be easy to recognize Jesus, even in a large crowd—just look for the most joyful person! *Father* anointed Jesus "with the oil of gladness beyond [his] companions" (Heb. 1:9). It is not surprising that Jesus frequently spoke about His own joy,[4] and once told His disciples that His joy is for them too: "That my joy may be in you and that your joy may be full" (John 15:11, 16:24).

> **IF YOU THINK OF JESUS AS STIFF, STERILE, POMPOUS, AUSTERE—THINK AGAIN.**

If you for a moment think *Father* does not have a good sense of humor, just consider the laughter that surrounded Abraham and the fulfillment of His promise of a family dynasty. No one re-tells the story better than Frederick Buechner.

> When God told Abraham, who was a hundred at the time, that at the age of ninety his wife Sarah was finally going to have a baby, Abraham came close to knocking himself out—"fell on his face and laughed." as Genesis puts it

(17:17). In another version of the story (18:8ff) Sarah is hiding behind the door eavesdropping, and here it's Sarah herself who nearly splits a gut although when God asks her about it afterward she denies it. "No, but you did laugh," God says, thus having the last word as well as the first. God doesn't seem to hold their outburst against them, however. On the contrary, he tells them the baby's going to be a boy and that he wants them to name him Isaac. Isaac in Hebrew means laughter.

Why did the two old crocks laugh? They laughed because they knew only a fool would believe that a woman with one foot in the grave was soon going to have her other foot in the maternity ward. They laughed because God expected them to believe it anyway. They laughed because God seemed to believe it. They laughed because they half-believed it themselves. They laughed because laughing felt better than crying. They laughed because if by some crazy chance it just happened to come true they would really have something to laugh about, and in the meanwhile it helped keep them going.[5]

If your view of Jesus sees Him stiff, sterile, pompous, austere, relationally challenged and socially awkward, think again. If He was stiff or aloof, He would never have been called the friend of drunks and sinners.[6] Jesus was not a wet blanket; He was the life of the party. One of my favorite moments in Jesus' life is when He, too, roared with laughter. As He welcomed home seventy-two mission-weary friends, and as they exchanged high-fives and fist pumps, the record shows, "Jesus rejoiced [*agalliao*] in the Holy Spirit" (Luke 10:21). *Agalliao* means to have super-infused joy, to rejoice exceedingly, and in this case, to rejoice supernaturally. Jesus laughed because *Father* laughs.

We have established that *Father* laughs, and Son laughs, but don't forget about the Holy Spirit—He too laughs. When it comes to joy, the Spirit does not come in third place. Not only is the Holy Spirit full of joy, He makes it possible for you, too, to be full of joy. The Bible talks about "joy in the Holy Spirit" (Rom. 14:17). The joyful Spirit wants to give you as much joy as He gave Jesus.

Sherpas

While oceanographers go deep, Sherpas go high. In fact, they live at an elevation few of us will ever reach even once in our lives. We have used the Mariana Trench as a word-picture for going deep into *Father's* love. Let's change the metaphor to change our perspective and make an equally important observation.

Sherpas live on the backside of the tallest mountain range on earth—the Himalayas. It is no stretch to suggest that the first time you take one look at *Father* and see yourself in vital union with Him, you will literally feel as though you are on top of the world. You will experience the breathtaking view of His love from a perspective that few other people have ever experienced. The view from above the clouds is not a random, once-in-a-lifetime view—not for a Sherpa. This is where they live. I have done my Sherpa research and discovered several fascinating features of this unique people group:

- Sherpas travel light—as light as possible.

- Sherpas don't just visit the heights; they live there.

- Sherpas don't just live in the mountains for themselves; they help others ascend.

- Sherpas strap themselves together with novice-climbers to keep them safe.

You and I as *Father*-seekers are Sherpa-like: We travel light—as light as possible; we don't just visit the heights, we live there; we help others ascend, and strap ourselves together with novice climbers to keep them safe. This may surprise you, but Sherpas are among the healthiest people on earth. Though they live in dangerous terrain and often experience brutally harsh weather conditions, they have developed a hyper-accelerated immune system that allows them to ward off many of the diseases that would threaten the average person. *Father* is calling you higher—He is calling you to be a Sherpa-seeker.

Unending Joy

When you step foot into *Father's* house, the first words you will hear will be, "Enter into the joy of the Lord" (Matt. 25:21, 23) because *Father's* house is a happy place. What makes this reality even more thrilling today is that *Father's* house and *Father's* joy don't start when we stop breathing; they start the moment we say *Abba, Daddy*.

King David looked forward to *Father's* house: "In your presence there is fullness of joy; at your right hand are pleasures forevermore" (Ps. 16:11). It is the manifest presence of *Father* and *Son* by the *Spirit* that give us the same fullness of joy today that we will have then. David ends the well-known Psalm 23 with the confident words which refer to the here and now: "Surely goodness and mercy shall follow me all the days of my life"; and he also ends the psalm with equally confident words referring to the hereafter: "And I will dwell in the house of the LORD forever" (23:6).

When your heart stops beating and your brain waves flat-line and *Father* welcomes you home, you will hear these words: "Enter into the joy of the Lord" (Matt. 25:21, 23). Heaven is described as the place where "everlasting joy shall be upon their heads" (Isa. 51:11). Joy characterizes His house because every new day in *Father*'s house will be even more joyful.

Re-parenting is joyful. *Father* will be re-parenting you forever, and there is no more joy-filled prayer than this:

Father, re-parent me in Jesus' name.

17

Father's Prayer

PRAYER IS AS natural as breathing in *Father's* house. Prayer is *Father's* language; when you are re-born and adopted as *Abba's* child, prayer becomes your heart-language also. The more you encounter *Father* now, the more at home you will be then.

Just Say Father is your introduction to the most significant relationship you will ever have. This may be the final chapter in the book, but hopefully it is only the first chapter of a new season in your life. Moving from orphan to adoption, from mask-wearing to mask-free living, from skimming across the surface to going deep, is the thrill of being *Abba's* child. You are now ready for the ride of your life.

Father-Time

It is now time to start spending time with *Father*—intentional, frequent, extended time—not to win favor but because you are favored; not to impress yourself but to express your passion; not because you're supposed to but because you want to. If you love Him, *Father*-time will become a highlight of your day. In fact, before you know it, *Father*-time will become so natural, as the default setting on your re-born spirit, sooner or later it will become one continuous flow of uninterrupted fellowship with Him. *Father*-time is the time each day you intentionally spend with *Father*. When we use the term, we are not referring to a grandfather clock or a fictional Disney character; we are talking about the time you spend with Him.

Jesus gave His disciples a tool to use as they built their *Father*-time. It has become known as the Lord's Prayer but would more appropriately be called *Father's* Prayer. Though given by Jesus, it was obviously not used by Jesus—*He* certainly did not need to ask for forgiveness from His trespasses, *we* do. We call it *Father's* Prayer because this is the realm in which we call on *Father*, and these are the words Jesus gave us to use.

> ## THE LORD'S PRAYER IS MORE THAN A PRAYER TO PRAY— IT'S A PATTERN TO FOLLOW.

It is likely Jesus gave this prayer multiple times, but *Father's* Prayer was recorded in the Bible on two separate occasions: both as a prayer to pray (see Luke 11:2–4) and as a pattern to follow (see Matt. 6:9–11). While used all over the world by Catholic, Protestant, Pentecostal, and Orthodox followers, few know exactly how to use it. Virtually everyone uses it as a prayer, but almost no one uses it as a pattern.

Saying it simply as a prayer can all too easily become mindless and ritualistic. You can take a deep breath and recite it from memory as a long run-on sentence without knowing what you're saying. For this reason, the prayer has even been discarded by some as a useless religious relic.

While useful as a prayer, as we will discover, it is ten times more effective to use it as a pattern. In fact, *Father's* Prayer is the greatest single re-parenting tool ever given.

Keep in mind, Jesus gave us this pattern to use as the structure for our *Father*-time. It contains all prayer and it is brilliantly structured. We have taught this seven-part pattern all over the world and it is being used to revive and ready the church.

1. Relationship—*Our Father who is in heaven*

2. Worship—*Hallowed be your name*

3. Lordship—*Your kingdom come, your will be done*

4. Sonship—*Give us this day our daily bread, and forgive us our debts*

5. Fellowship—*As we also have forgiven our debtors*

6. Leadership—*And lead us not into temptation, but deliver us from the evil one*

7. Ownership—*For yours is the kingdom and the power and the glory, forever.*[1]

As we have said, *Father's* Prayer is the best re-parenting tool ever given. This prayer is a primer to help you structure your *Father*-time in a meaningful and effective way. While re-parenting will last for all eternity, *Father* wants you to start now.

Jesus said His *Father's* house is a house of prayer, and it only makes sense that the seven parts of *Father's* Prayer represent the seven rooms in *Father's* house. This word picture of the seven rooms in *Father's* house is a dynamic way to remember the seven sequential parts to *Father's* Prayer. If you love *Father*, you certainly love His presence, and you will encounter His presence in every room in His house.

1. *Father*'s Prayer appropriately starts "Our *Father*," and the first room in *Father*'s house is called *Relationship*. In a sense this is the lobby or entryway of *Father*'s house. It is here where you welcome *Father* and where you are welcomed by *Father*. He immediately greets you with His radical love and blessing. He wants you to know every day that you are not an orphan or a street beggar; you are an adopted child, blessed and highly favored. In Christ, you now have the right to call Him *Abba, Daddy, Papa*. Spending time in the entryway of *Father*'s house should be the highlight of your day, and the love you receive in this first room goes with you into every room.

2. The second room in *Father*'s house is called *Worship*— "Hallowed be your name." All worship is in response to God's name. This is the room in *Father*'s house with the tallest ceiling, because the Bible says, "The name of the LORD is a strong tower" (Prov. 18:10). This is where you encounter the greatness of His name. *Father*'s name is *Father*'s character—His supremacy, sufficience, potency, and majesty. As you declare the supremacy of God's name, you clear the spiritual atmosphere and airspace above you. The name you declare in this second room touches every room in the house.

3. The third room in *Father*'s house is called *Lordship*— "your Kingdom come, your will be done." Out of the *Father*'s name in room two, you now enter the third room where you receive His kingdom. When you pray the kingdom, you are praying the Holy Spirit because only the Holy Spirit can bring the rule and reign of God on earth. *Father*'s book says that the kingdom of God is, "righteousness and peace and joy in the Holy Spirit" (Rom. 14:17). *Father*'s kingdom is full of repentance, healing, salvation, revelation, righteousness, joy, and peace.

4. The fourth room in *Father's* house is *Sonship*—"give us this day our daily bread, and forgive us our debts." The fourth room is right in the middle of the seven rooms, and it is here in the heart of the house where God meets all your needs—your physical needs, represented by daily bread, and your spiritual needs, represented by forgiveness. This is where *Father* brings home the groceries, give us today our daily bread, and takes out the garbage, forgive us our sins.

5. The fifth room is called *Fellowship*—"as we also have forgiven our debtors." In order to maintain healthy relationship between family members, it is essential to extend forgiveness. *Father* wants us to consistently pause in room five. This is a most important room for all of us. The quickest way to become like Christ is to forgive like Christ. While forgiveness doesn't minimize the offense nor deny the pain, it is a choice that says, "I will not hurt you even though you hurt me."

6. The sixth room in *Father's* house is *Leadership*—"lead us not into temptation, but deliver us from the evil one." You and I have two primary enemies—the enemy within which is sin, and the Enemy without which is Satan. This sixth room is the war room in which we ask *Father* to give us victory over both our enemies. In a sense, the entire prayer builds to this sixth room where we learn to exercise our authority in Christ.

7. The seventh and final room in *Father's* house is called *Ownership*—"for yours is the kingdom and the power and the glory forever." Before you finish your *Father*-time, it is important to declare His ownership over all things. In the first six rooms of *Father's* house, you receive one blessing after another, and now, before you leave *Father's* house, you want to pause and give it all back to Him.

Father's Prayer, as we have said, is the best re-parenting tool ever given. "Our *Father* in heaven" expresses your identity as daughters and sons, and you receive His blessing of acceptance, affection, affirmation and significance in the first room of His house. "Hallowed be your name" declares the supremacy of Christ and takes hold of your identity, authority, and dignity in Him in the second room. "Your kingdom come" calls for the Kingdom on earth by the power of the Holy Spirit in the third room. "Give us this day our daily bread" receives food, and "forgive us our debts" receives forgiveness in the fourth room. "As we also have forgiven our debtors" extends forgiveness in the fifth room. "Lead us not into temptation" declares your victory over sin, and "deliver us from the evil one" declares your victory over Satan in the sixth room. "Yours is the kingdom, and the power, and the glory, forever" affirms *Father's* ownership over all things. The collective impact of this prayer will be felt for all eternity.

Peel the Banana

I had flown twenty-eight hours from Atlanta to India, and I was bone tired. I checked into my guest room, took a long shower, and brushed the moss off my teeth. I got six hours of sleep that felt more like a power nap than a full night's sleep, and yet was wide awake at 3 a.m. I was experiencing a full-blown case of jet lag. I was scheduled to teach *Father's* Prayer in six hours, and as a person who does not like to waste time, I began thinking how to contextualize my talk.

For some reason, I kept envisioning a cluster of bananas, and suddenly it dawned on me—the bananas were a perfect picture of the problem with *Father's* Prayer. As I stood behind the lectern in front of an auditorium full of eager faces a few hours later, I greeted the polite crowd, peeled my banana, and took a big bite. "I want to talk with you this morning about *Father's* Prayer pattern," I announced as I realized talking with a mouthful of banana was harder than I expected; but my playful sense of humor made the best of it.

As I quoted *Father's* Prayer, I took a second bite and announced, "This banana is delicious, moist, nutritious." The crowd began to chuckle as I continued, "The only problem with *Father's* Prayer is that we have made it religious. Neither Catholics, Protestants, Orthodox, nor Pentecostals know what to do with it," I said as I finished my banana.

> ## REMOVE THE RELIGIOUS BANANA PEEL FROM *FATHER'S* PRAYER—AND EAT THE BANANA!

I was now holding nothing but a banana peel. "We have made *Father's* Prayer so religious, so formal, so predictable, we have completely missed the point. Like this banana peel, *Father's* Prayer has become bitter, dry, and sickening to eat. My friends, it's time to remove the religious banana peel from *Father's* Prayer and throw it away. Because we need the banana!"

My Indian friends began to shout, whistle, clap, and cheer. They obviously got the point, and I proceeded to teach them what I have presented to you.

They were not clapping at the banana; they were clapping at the word picture that made perfect sense to them. They had been biting into the religious banana peel of *Father's* Prayer, and assumed the prayer was dry and bitter: but now they were ready to sink their teeth into the moist, sweet, nutritious part of *Father's* Prayer, and I hope you are too.

I Am

The more time you spend with *Father*, the less time you spend looking at your watch. *Father*-time is not a matter of punching a time clock; it's about centering your soul. Your *Father*-time is what gives significance and meaning to all the other moments of life. A simple string holds together pearls so they form a beautiful necklace, and your *Father*-time gives perfect sequence and symmetry to the complexities of life. In fact, your *Father*-time is what enables you to maximize every other moment, and thoroughly enjoy them all. Let me explain.

When *Father* was asked His name, He replied, "I AM WHO I AM" (Exod. 3:14). This curious answer provides a warehouse full of insight into *Father's* nature. It points to His ever-present existence and His ever-present being—both the noun and the verb of being. The noun "I" in *I AM* shows *Father's* continual state of existence, and the verb "AM" in *I AM* shows His perpetual state of action. It's not surprising John Piper calls this verse, "The most important text in all the Bible for understanding the meaning of the name Yahweh."[2]

Father is the essence of being, and He lives in the perpetual present. As the only non-created Being, He is eternal, and I AM WHO I AM is a spot-on way to identify Himself. Unlike anyone else, *Father* has no regrets about the past nor fears about the future; He is eternally free to live now and enjoy every moment. One of the collateral benefits of being *Abba's* child is that He gives you the same ability—He teaches you to live in the moment and enjoy every experience along the way.

Satan sits in stark contrast. He is completely locked out of the present and unable to enjoy the moment. In the final part of *Father's* book, Satan incarnate, the one who will be known as the beast, is described three times as the one who, "Was and is not and is to come" (Rev. 17:8, 9, 10). Think about it slowly: He was and is not and is to come; i.e., Satan lives in a constant state of regret over the past, in dread of his future, and totally unable to enjoy the moment. While he promises momentary pleasure and instant gratification, he is a liar: he is unable to deliver an ounce of true satisfaction, because he *IS NOT*. What a contrast to *I AM!*

Father, on the other hand, lives in the moment as the I AM WHO I AM. As *Abba's* child, you, too, will learn to maximize the moment and enjoy every experience. Regardless of the challenges and opportunities you face from this day forward, you can be confident that *Father* is with you—blessing, loving, healing, and redeeming you.

By now you most likely realize that our six-word prayer is much more than a prayer; it's a disposition or an orientation of the heart. Re-parenting reverses the aging process. In the kingdom, the older you get, the younger you get—the less childish and the more childlike; the less independent and the more dependent; the less predictable and the more playful and creative; the less brittle and the more flexible; the less distracted and the more captivated. Parenting is another word for well-being, mentoring, or spiritual formation. Re-parenting has been *Father's* endgame from the beginning; it's also the finish line toward which all history is moving. What began the moment of your re-birth and spirit adoption will never end. What began in the shallows will take you to the Mariana Trench. You outgrow diapers and training wheels, but you will never outgrow this prayer:

Father, re-parent me in Jesus' name.

Small-Group Study Guide

YOUR *FATHER* JOURNEY is one that starts solo and always leads to family. While your private *Father* encounters are significant and relevant, your corporate *Father* encounters are too. The healthier your heart, the more frequently you will gather with others in the family to encounter Him.

This *Just Say Father* Small-Group Study Guide is designed not simply to provide you with key questions to stimulate your thinking, but more importantly to help you build an environment where you authentically meet with *Father* together.

You will need to decide how many weeks you want your study to last. This Study Guide has been prepared for eight weeks, but you can adapt it to move along more quickly in four weeks (take two sessions per week) or more slowly in sixteen weeks. You decide what works best for you and your people. These eight sessions have been structured to essentially cover two chapters per session.

Healthy Group Guidelines

Everyone's *Father* journey is sacred, and everyone in the group is special. Everyone has a different starting point in the journey, and you will want to keep that in mind.

Honor—You want to treat everyone with honor and respect, regardless of where they are in their journey. You do not want to tolerate rejection, judgmentalism, or disrespect as these bad attitudes are contrary to *Father*'s heart.

Listen—You always want to try to hear from everyone in the group. While you don't want to force anyone to speak, you want to ask simple and provocative questions that everyone can answer.

Thought-provoking—Several of the questions are thinking questions designed to stimulate intellectually satisfying responses.

Heart questions—Some questions are designed for application, and some for emotional vulnerability.

Encounter—The key to your *Just Say Father* small group is encountering the *Father*. The goal of the group is not simply to talk about Him but to encounter Him. It would be a travesty to meet together with each other week after week and fail to encounter *Father*.

Be creative—*Father* is creative, and He made you to be creative. No one knows your group better than you and *Father*. Ask Him for wisdom in how to facilitate your small group.

Listen—He will counsel you. You can count on it!

Session One
Chapter 1: *Father*

We recommend asking someone in the group to lead in prayer. Invite *Father* God to make Himself known to each one in the group as you meet together. You can find many wonderful *Father* songs on YouTube that you may want to play some time during your meeting.

1. What did you learn about *Father* in chapter one? Take your time. Listen carefully to each comment.

2. What did you learn about yourself in chapter one? Take your time. Listen carefully.

3. Respond to the statement, "*Father* is the solitary name that captures both the complexity and the simplicity of God."

4. Why do you think rock music is full of this father-thing? Be specific. Be personal. With what father-songs or father-wounds can you identify?

5. How do you respond to the idea of being re-parented by God?

6. What parallels do you notice between Simba's journey in *The Lion King* and your own journey with *Father*?

7. Discuss the suggested prayer: "*Father*, re-parent me in Jesus name." How do you initially respond to this prayer?

As you conclude this first session, remind everyone of the purpose of your group: to encounter *Father* and to get to know Him by experience. End your meeting with prayer. Call on someone to pray or ask everyone to pray a brief prayer going around the circle clockwise, completing the sentence, "*Father*, thank you for…"

Session Two
Chapter 2: *Father's Heart*
Chapter 3: *Father's Hurt*

Remember: always invite *Father* God to make Himself known to each one in the group. You may choose to play a *Father* song as well.

1. What words would you use to describe *Father's* heart?

2. Respond to the statement, "Inside *Father's* heart is where you first existed."

3. What are some similarities and differences between your heart and *Father's* heart?

4. What does it mean to know *Father* by heart?

5. In what way does *Father* hurt?

6. How does Fred Peppermen illustrate *Father*?

7. How would you describe the difference between *Father* and the father of lies?

As you conclude your second session, remind everyone of the purpose of your group: to encounter *Father* and to get to know Him by experience. End your meeting with prayer. Call on someone to pray or ask everyone to pray a brief prayer going around the circle clockwise, completing the sentence, "*Father*, I appreciate you because…"

Session Three
Chapter 4: *Father's Son*
Chapter 5: *Father's Orphans*

Remember: always invite *Father* God to make Himself known to each one in the group. You may choose to play a *Father* song as well.

1. What words can you use to accurately describe Jesus' unique relationship with *Father*?

2. What is the meaning of the Greek word *monogenes*? What does this word tell us about Jesus?

3. What is the meaning of the Greek word *exegeomai*? What does this word tell us about Jesus?

4. What is the significance of the words of Jesus from the cross, "*Eli, Eli, lema sabachthani*," or "My God, My God, why have you forsaken me"?

5. List several ways in which the cross of Jesus is a scandal.

6. What did you learn in chapter 5 about orphans? About the orphan spirit?

7. What does God's name "*Father* of the fatherless" mean to you?

As you conclude your second session, remind everyone of the purpose of your group: to encounter *Father* and to get to know Him by experience. End your meeting with prayer. Call on someone to pray or ask everyone to pray a brief prayer going around the circle clockwise, completing the sentence, "*Father*, thank you for sending Your Son Jesus because…"

Session Four
Chapter 6: *Father's Adoption*
Chapter 7: *Father's Child*

Remember: always invite *Father* God to make Himself known to each one in the group. You may choose to play a *Father* song as well.

1. What do Jesus' words, "I will not leave you as orphans," mean to you?

2. Compare the similarities and differences between orphans and spirit-orphans.

3. What is the meaning of the Greek word *huiothesia*? What does it mean to you?

4. Describe the similarities and distinctives between spirit adoption and spirit re-birth.

5. What struck you from the story about the wealthy man's estate and the gardener?

6. What evidence of the orphan spirit have you seen in your life? Be specific.

7. What did you learn about the difference between childlike and childish? What evidences of childlikeness have you seen in the life of a *Father*-follower whom you admire?

Remind everyone of the purpose of your group: to encounter *Father* and to get to know Him by experience. As you end your meeting today in prayer, encourage everyone to pray a short prayer of appreciation to *Father* for your adoption and your re-birth.

Session Five
Chapter 8: *Father's Love*
Chapter 9: *Father's Ear*
Chapter 10: *Father's Voice*

Remember: always invite *Father* God to make Himself known to each one in the group. You may choose to play a *Father* song as well.

1. How has God begun to heal your love receptors? Be specific.

2. Chapter eight contains two significant declarations—one to heal your love receptors, and the other to receive a Holy Spirit love infusion. Explain which, if any, of these declarations were beneficial to you.

3. In what way is *Father's* love a battle cry? Have you ever used His love as a war cry?

4. How has *Father* encouraged your prayer life while reading this book? Give an example of prayer growth. Be specific.

5. What did you learn about *Father* in the story told by Dr. Roseveare about the orphaned newborn and two-year-old?

6. How did chapter 10 help you better hear God's voice? Be specific. Give an example of something you have heard *Father* say to you?

7. What does it mean to you to keep secrets with God? For Him to keep secrets with you?

Remind the group of your purpose: to encounter *Father* and to get to know Him by experience. As you end your meeting today, consider taking a risk: sit in silence for one minute as you listen to what *Father* says to you personally. Then give a few minutes for people to say exactly what they heard Him say to them. This could be a significant exercise.

Session Six
Chapter 11: *Father's Blessing*
Chapter 12: *Father's Healing*

Remember: always invite *Father* God to make Himself known to each one in the group. You may choose to play a *Father* song as well.

1. Name and describe the three distinctives included in the *Father's* blessing.

2. Which of these three distinct blessings have you experienced? Be specific.

3. How does the *Father's* blessing become a family blessing? Give an example of a family blessing you have noticed in someone else's family.

4. How have you experienced *Father's* healing? Be specific.

5. In what area of your life do you yet need *Father's* healing? Be honest and specific.

6. Have you ever experienced an "infected wound" as described in chapter 12? Be specific.

7. Respond to the statement, "*Father's* love is the greatest force on earth."

Remind the group of your purpose: to encounter *Father* and to get to know Him by experience. As you end your meeting today, hold out your hands to *Father* and thank Him for His blessings. Then ask, "Does anyone in the group want specific prayer for healing on some level?"

Session Seven
Chapter 13: *Father's Identity*
Chapter 14: *Father's Calling*

Remember: always invite *Father* God to make Himself known to each one in the group. You may choose to play a *Father* song as well.

1. Respond to the statement, "When you find *Father*, you get two for one—you find Him and you find yourself."

2. Respond to the statement, "Low self-esteem is the curse of our species; *Father* is the cure."

3. Can you relate to the story the author told about the day he realized he had an I-doll in his heart? Be specific.

4. What did you learn about your calling? Be specific.

5. Define the distinction between your identity and your calling? What is the connection between the two?

6. What impressed you about the difference between your calling and your assignment? Be specific.

7. What does it take for you to experience genuine fulfillment in life, and how does *Father* effect your fulfillment?

Remember: the purpose of our group is to encounter *Father* and to get to know Him by experience. We want to take time right now to worship Him and to validate each other's identity and calling.

Session Eight
Chapter 15: *Father's House*
Chapter 16: *Father's Joy*
Chapter 17: *Father's Prayer*

This is our final meeting. We have each received many blessings through our study. Let's take time as we begin this session for each of us to thank *Father* for specific benefits He has given us over the past several weeks.

1. How did your view of heaven change as you read chapter 15? Be specific.

2. What surprises can you expect in heaven?

3. Were you surprised to learn *Father* laughs? Why or why not?

4. Unending joy is a good description of *Father's* house. Why? What does this mean to you?

5. Why is it true that all too often prayer becomes boring? Why should prayer never be boring?

6. What new insight did you gain about *Father's* Prayer? Be specific. Take time with this question.

7. As you finish your study, discuss the value of this six-word prayer, "*Father*, re-parent me in Jesus name."

As you know, the purpose of our group has been to encounter *Father* and get to know Him by experience. Has our group been successful in accomplishing this purpose? Before you talk to *Father*, talk to each other. Answer this question: What specific benefits have you received during our study?

Now take time to talk to *Father*. Thank Him for each of His benefits.

End your final session by praying in your own words our six-word prayer, "*Father*, re-parent me in Jesus name."

Notes

Introduction

1. John Arnott, *The Father's Blessing* (Lake Mary, FL: Creation House, 1997).
2. John Eldridge, *Fathered by God* (Nashville: Thomas Nelson, 2009).
3. John Fisher, *Twelve Steps to the Recovering Pharisee* (Minneapolis: Bethany House, 2000).
4. Richard J Foster, *Celebration of Discipline: The Path to Spiritual Growth* (San Francisco: Harper & Row, 1988).
5. Richard J Foster, *Prayer: Finding the Heart's True Home* (San Francisco: HarperCollins, 1992).
6. Jack Frost, *Experiencing Father's Embrace* (Shippensburg, PA: Destiny Image, 2002).
7. Jack Frost, *Spiritual Slavery to Spiritual Sonship* (Shippensburg, PA: Destiny Image, 2006).
8. Tim Keller, *Prodigal God* (New York: Penguin, 2008).
9. Brennan Manning, *Abba's Child* (Colorado Springs: Navpress, 2015).
10. D. Martyn-Lloyd Jones, *Romans (Chapter 8:5–17) The Sons of God* (Carlisle, PA: The Banner of Truth Trust, 1974).
11. Donald Miller, *To Own a Dragon* (Colorado Springs: Navpress, 2006).
12. Henri Nouwen, *The Return of the Prodigal Son* (New York: Doubleday, 1994).
13. John Piper, *Desiring God* (New York: Penguin, 1986).
14. John Piper, *The Pleasures of God* (New York: Penguin, 2012).
15. Thomas A. Smail, *The Forgotten Father* (Eugene, OR: Wipf and Stock Publishers, 1980).
16. Gary Smalley and John Trent, *The Blessing* (New York: Pocket Books, 1986).
17. Mark Stibbe, *From Orphans to Heirs* (Oxford: The Bible Reading Fellowship, 1999).

Chapter 1: Father

1. Justin Bieber, "Where Are U Now" (OWSLA, 2015).
2. Christina Aguilera, "Hurt" (RCA, 2006).
3. U2, "Sometimes You Can't Make It On Your Own" (Island, Interscope, 2005).
4. Eric Clapton, "My Father's Eyes" (Reprise, 1998).
5. Tom Wolfe, *The Story of a Novel* (New York: Charles A. Scribners, 1964).
6. John Eldridge, *Fathered by God*, 11.
7. Donald Miller, 68.
8. Donald Miller, 72.
9. Disney, *The Lion King* (Walt Disney Company, 1994).

Chapter 2: Father's Heart

1. Richard J. Foster, *Prayer: Finding the Heart's True Home*, 85.
2. This is the famous passage from St. Augustine's *Confessions* (Lib 1, 1–2, 2.5, 5: CSEL 33, 1–5).
3. Henry Scougal, *The Life of God in the Soul of Man* (Minneapolis: Bethany Fellowship, 1976), 13.
4. Scougal, 62–63.
5. Mother Teresa, *Where There is Love, There is God: A Path to Closer Union with God and Greater Love* (New York: Doubleday, 2010).
6. Mother Teresa, *Where There is Love, There is God*.
7. Sarah Hopkins Bradford, *Scenes in the Life of Harriet Tubman* (Auburn, NY: 2018).
8. Acts 13:22.
9. 1 John 4:8, 16.
10. John 13:34, 35; 15:12, 17.
11. John 21:15–17.
12. John 13:23, 25.

Chapter 3: Father's Hurt

1. John Lennon, "Mother" (Lennon Music, Lenono Music, 1970).
2. Psalm 78:38; 86:15; 111:4; 112:4; 145:8.

3. Rachel Paula Abrahamson, "Dad drowns saving his daughters from riptide while vacationing in Florida." (*Today Show*, 2019) https://www.today.com/parents/dad-drowns-saving-his-daughters-riptide-florida-t159420.

4. Julie Meunier Pepperman. (2019, July 15) https://www.facebook.com/julie.pepperman [Facebook Update].

5. Brittany Crocker, "Fred Pepperman's love story began in 1987 and lives on through the daughters he died saving." (2019) from https://www.knoxnews.com/story/news/2019/07/26/maryville-father-live-through-daughters-he-died-save/1824550001/.

6. Brittany Crocker.

7. Brittany Crocker.

8. Brittany Crocker.

Chapter 4: Father's Son

1. Matthew 9:36; 14:14; 15:32; 20:34; Mark 1:41; 6:34; 8:2; Luke 7:13; 10:33.

2. Luke 23:44–45.

3. John 12:26; 14:11

4. John 14:13; 15:9; Luke 3:22.

5. John 6:32; 17:11, 21; 11:14; 14:6; 15:16; 16:23, 26; 20:21.

6. John 6:57; 8:16; Luke 22:29; John 5:37; 12:49; 16:22.

7. Luke 4:18–19.

8. John 14:13; 15:9; 10:18; Luke 22:42.

Chapter 5: Father's Orphans

1. UNICEF, "Orphans," 2017 https://www.unicef.org/media/media_45279.html.

2. Reba McEntire, "The Greatest Man I Never Knew" (Emi April Music Inc., Lion-hearted Music, 1991).

3. Jack Frost, *Spiritual Slavery to Spiritual Sonship*, 37.

4. Jack Frost, 38.

5. John Eldridge, *Fathered by God*, 29.

6. Edward Davis, "Anne Hathaway on Channeling her tears, emotions, and cutting her hair for harrowing Les Misérables scene"

(2012). https://www.indiewire.com/2012/12/anne-hathaway-on-channeling-her-tears-emotions-cutting-her-hair-for-harrowing-les-miserables-scene-249973/.

7. "I Dreamed a Dream," *Les Miserables* (Warner Chappell Music, 2014).

8. Lesley Messer, "Anne Hathaway says she faked happiness when she won her Oscar" (2016). https://abcnews.go.com/Entertainment/anne-hathaway-admits-faked-happiness-won-oscar/story?id=42971169.

9. Tim Anderson, "Marilyn Monroe, Steve Jobs, and 6 Other Famous Orphans Who Changed the World" (2019). https://owlcation.com/humanities/Eight-Famous-People-You-Didnt-Know-Were-Orphans.

10. Helen Colton, *The Gift of Touch* (New York: Seaview/Putnam, 1983), 49.

11. Tim Anderson.

12. James Finley, *Merton's Palace of Nowhere: A Search for God Through Awareness of the True Self* (Notre Dame, IN: Ave Maria Press, 1978), 53.

13. Tim Keller, 53.

14. Paige Pichler, "What you need to know about Dennis Rodman's Kids" (2020). https://www.thelist.com/230890/what-you-need-to-know-about-dennis-rodmans-kids/.

15. Paige Pichler.

16. Paige Pichler.

17. Paige Pichler.

18. Paige Pichler.

19. Paige Pichler.

Chapter 6: Father's Adoption

1. Life Is Beautiful Ministries of Faith, "36 Shocking Statistics on Fatherless Homes" (October 4, 2018) https://lifeisbeautiful.org/statistics-on-fatherless-homes/.

2. Life Is Beautiful Ministries of Faith.

3. Bob Dylan, "Like a Rolling Stone" (Universal Music Publishing Group, 1965).
4. Simon Tugwell, *The Beatitudes: Soundings in Christian Tradition* (Springfield, IL: Templegate, 1980), 130.
5. J.I. Packer, *Knowing God* (London: Hodder & Stoughton, 1993), 232.
6. http://www.jaredstory.com/story_of_a_son.html.
7. Jay Z/Blue Ivy Carter/Shawn Carter/Pharrell Williams, "Glory." Sony/ATV Music Publishing LLC, Warner Chappell Music, Inc, Songtrust Ave, 2012.

Chapter 7: Father's Child

1. Jack Frost, *Spiritual Slavery to Spiritual Sonship*, 38.
2. https://www.mayoclinic.org/diseases-conditions/reactive-attach-ment-disorder/symptoms-causes/syc-20352939.
3. Jack Frost, 132-198.
4. Charles Spurgeon, *On Revival*, quoted in Mark Stibbe, 27.
5. Brennan Manning, *Abba's Child* (Colorado Springs: Navpress, 2015), 76.
6. Frederick Buechner, *The Magnificent Defeat* (San Francisco, CA: Harper & Row, 1966), 135.

Chapter 8: Father's Love

1. Ephesians 4:30.
2. 1 Corinthians 12:7.
3. 1 Corinthians 2:16.
4. R.A. Torrey, *The Holy Spirit* (Old Tappan, NJ: Revell 1977), 11.
5. Quoted in J. Armstrong, *Five Great Evangelists* (Christian Focus Publications, 1997), 132-133.
6. Frederick Lehman, "The Love of God is Greater Far" (hymn, words and music), 1923.
7. Jonathan David Helser/Melissa Helser/Molly Skaggs/Jake Stevens, "Raise a Hallelujah." Bethel Music Publishing, 2019.
8. Jessica Lea, "How a 2-Year-Old's Miracle Inspired a Crazy Popular Bethel Praise Song," (2019). https://churchleaders.com/pastors/

videos-for-pastors/344645-how-a-2-year-olds-miracle-inspired-a-crazy-popular-bethel-praise-song.html.

9. Kriza Jo L. Tandunyan, "The Powerful Testimony Behind Bethel Music's New Song 'Raise a Hallelujah,'" https://godtv.com/the-powerful-testimony-behind-bethel-musics-new-song-raise-a-hallelujah/#:~:text=The%20testimony%20of%20the%20song,transfusions%20and%20go%20on%20dialysis.

Chapter 9: Father's Ear

1. Harry Chapin, "Cat's in the Cradle" (Elektra, 1974).

2. Richard J. Foster, *Prayer: Finding the Heart's True Home.*

3. The Lord's Prayer Pattern is the most foundational, all-inclusive prayer ever written, and the only prayer given to *Father* followers by Jesus. The seven parts of the Lord's Prayer correspond to seven rooms in the house of prayer, as taught throughout the world by the College of Prayer. These seven rooms in the house of prayer are as follows: *Relationship*—Our *Father*; *Worship*—hallowed be your name; *Lordship*—your kingdom come, your will be done; *Sonship*—give us . . . forgive us; *Fellowship*—as we forgive others; *Leadership*—lead us not . . . but deliver us; *Ownership*—yours is the kingdom, power, and glory. Of the seven rooms in the house of prayer, every room reflects the presence of *Father*, and fosters and ever deepening love relationship. For further insight into this strategic prayer pattern, visit collegeofprayer.org and download the app, Revival Now Media.

4. Helen Roseveare, *Living Faith* (Christian Focus Publications, 1980).

Chapter 10: Father's Voice

1. Matthew 6:4.

2. Matthew 6:6.

3. Matthew 6:18.

Chapter 11: Father's Blessing

1. Thomas Merton, *The New Man* (New York: Farrar, Straus & Giroux, 1999).
2. Madonna, "Papa Don't Preach" (Sire, Warner Bros, 1986).
3. Thomas Merton, *The Hidden Ground of Love: Letter* (New York: Farrar, Straus & Giroux, 1985), 146.

Chapter 12: Father's Healing

1. Richard J. Foster, Prayer: Finding the Heart's True Home, 1.
2. Paul Simon, "The Boxer" (Paul Simon Music, Warner/Chappell Music Ltd, 1968).
3. Fred Hartley III, *The Seven Wounds of Christ: Where Skeptics, Cynics and Seekers Find Unexpected Healing* (Fort Washington, PA: CLC Publications, 2017).

Chapter 13: Father's Identity

1. Bob Dylan, "Abandoned Love" (Ram's Horn Music, 1975).
2. Bob Dylan, "Ain't No Man Righteous No Not One" (Special Rider Music, 1981).
3. Brennan Manning, *Abba's Child*, xv–xvi.
4. Henri J.M. Nouwen, *Life of the Beloved: Spiritual Living in a Secular World* (New York: Crossroad, 1992), 21.
5. Brennan Manning, *Abba's Child*, xv.
6. Brennan Manning, *Abba's Child*, xvii.
7. James Finley, *Merton's Palace of Nowhere: A Search for God Through Awareness of the True Self* (Notre Dame: Ave Maria Press, 1978), 96.
8. Brennan Manning, *Abba's Child*, 105.

Chapter 14: Father's Calling

1. Brennan Manning, *Abba's Child*, 20.
2. Nouwen, *Life of the Beloved*, 34.
3. Nouwen, *Life of the Beloved*, 107.
4. Nouwen, *Life of the Beloved*, 127.

5. Brennan Manning, *Abba's Child*, 44.

6. Mother Teresa, *Where There Is Love, There Is God* (New York: Random House 2010), 4.

Chapter 15: Father's House

1. Richard Hoffer, "What Bo Knows Now," *Sports Illustrated*, October 30, 1995, 56.

2. Richard Hoffer, 56.

3. Richard Hoffer, 57.

4. Kesha, "Father Daughter Dance" (Spirit Music Group, 2020).

5. John 15:9.

6. John 15:12.

7. Charles Spurgeon, *On Revival*, 26.

Chapter 16: Father's Joy

1. John Piper, *The Pleasures of God* (New York: Penguin, 2012), xv.

2. Psalms 2:4; 37:13; 59:6; Lamentations 1:7; Job 39:22; 41:29.

3. 2 Samuel 6:5, 21; 1 Chronicles 13:8.

4. John 3:29; 15:11; 17:13.

5. Frederick Buechner, *Wishful Thinking: A Theological ABC* (New York, NY: Harper & Row, 1973), 24–45.

6. Matthew 11:19.

Chapter 17: Father's Prayer

1. For the PDF version of *Father*'s Prayer, visit collegeofprayer.org or the app Revival Now Media. It is available as a bookmark or booklet, along with many other useful resources.

2. John Piper, "I Am Who I Am" (Sermon, Bethlehem Baptist Church, Minneapolis, MN, September 16, 1984), Desiring God, https://www.desiringgod.org/messages/i-am-who-i-am.

PUBLICATIONS

Fort Washington, PA 19034

This book is published by CLC Publications, an outreach of CLC Ministries International. The purpose of CLC is to make evangelical Christian literature available to all nations so that people may come to faith and maturity in the Lord Jesus Christ. We hope this book has been life changing and has enriched your walk with God through the work of the Holy Spirit. If you would like to know more about CLC, we invite you to visit our website:

www.clcusa.org

To know more about the remarkable story of the founding
of CLC International, we encourage you to read

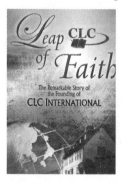

LEAP OF FAITH

Norman Grubb

Paperback
Size 5^1/$_4$ x 8, Pages 248
ISBN: 978-0-87508-650-7
ISBN (*e-book*): 978-1-61958-055-8

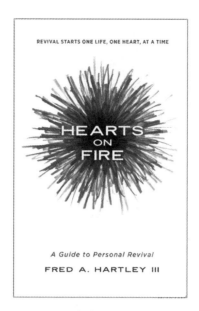

REVIVAL STARTS ONE LIFE, ONE HEART, AT A TIME

A Guide to Personal Revival

FRED A. HARTLEY III

HEARTS on FIRE
A Guide to Personal Revival
REVIVAL STARTS ONE HEART, ONE LIFE AT A TIME

Fred A. Hartley III

Heart-fire is the invigorating feeling that ignites inside you when you encounter the reality of the living God—and the effect is spontaneous combustion! God wants to set your heart on fire and make you a history-shaper. This is not a book *about* revival, it's a book *of* revival. *Small Group Study Guide included.*

Paperback
Size 5¹/₄ x 8, Pages 250
ISBN: 978-1-61958-322-1
ISBN (*e-book*): 978-1-61958-323-8

IGNITE
CARRYING THE FLAME FROM THE UPPER ROOM TO THE NATIONS
IGNITING A PRAYER MOVEMENT
to Reach the Final Unreached People on Earth

Fred A. Hartley III

The remaining unreached people on earth will not be reached by a lukewarm church; it will take a prayer-filled and Christ-filled church. *Ignite* is brimming with kingdom-building prayer principles that have stood the test of time. Explore the five Upper Room miracles that are the marks of every healthy church; and learn field-tested strategies to mobilize missional prayer in your church, your family, and your own life. *Group Prayer Guide included.*

Paperback
Size 5¹/₄ x 8, Pages 143
ISBN: 978-1-61958-308-5
ISBN (*e-book*): 978-1-61958-309-2

GOD ON FIRE
Encountering the Manifest Presence of Christ

Fred A. Hartley III

As believers, we are more alive in the middle of God's white-hot presence than anywhere else on earth. The history of revival is often studied from man's perspective; what we do to encounter God. *God on Fire* explores what God does to encounter us.

Paperback
Size 5 ¼ x 8, Pages 206
ISBN 978-1-61958-012-1
ISBN (*e-book*) 978-1-61958-066-4